THE
SOCIAL
BABY

Lynne Murray and Liz Andrews

Edited by Sue Parish

CP Publishing

To our children – Joe, Tim, Ilan and Hallam,
Sofie and Josh, who have taught us so much.

First published in 2000 by CP Publishing
Richmond, Surrey, United Kingdom

Text Copyright © 2000 Lynne Murray
This edition Copyright © 2000 The Children's Project Ltd

Edited by Sue Parish
Designed by Clive Dorman

ISBN 1 903275 01 6

Printed in Hong Kong

CONTENTS

THE CHILDREN'S PROJECT & THE SOCIAL BABY

We founded the Children's Project following the birth of our daughter Hannah in 1993. The family includes two older boys, Charlie and Barney, from a previous marriage.

Hannah was very much a wanted baby and we both felt well read and well prepared for the arrival of our new baby. In reality, neither of us was remotely prepared for the impact this new arrival had on both of us. Unlike the two boys, Hannah was what we have come to learn to call, a 'sensitive' child.

During the first weeks and months we experienced many unexpected emotional and physical challenges which prompted us to ask exactly how we should cope with, and understand, our baby. Talking to friends and family made us realise that, far from being unusual, our experience was much closer to the norm. The heart of the issue seemed to be a combination of factors that happens once a baby arrives. Whilst it is true to say that babies are born into a widely varying range of circumstances – cultural, economical and circumstantial – all parents need support and answers to questions at some time. Modern western culture seems superficially to be focussed almost entirely upon the pursuit of material possessions and success, and it is not always easy to find answers to questions about babies and small children. Indeed, every question seems to result in many different and often conflicting answers. The more we spoke with parents, the more we realised the extent of the need for something that could supply answers and offer support. This became our *raison d'être* for The Children's Project and *The Social Baby*.

The Children's Project believes that supporting parents and helping them to understand and communicate with their baby from birth can only have a positive effect on the relationship between the parents and the developing child. In the long term, any reduction in conflict between parent and child can only have a beneficial effect on that child, and ultimately on our society.

As parents, we knew we could not make sweeping statements, so we began to approach professionals to see if they would support our views. After a long 'journey' we were introduced to Professor Lynne Murray, co-director of the Winnicott Research Unit, University of Reading, UK, who has a wealth of experience in studying mother/infant relationships. Some three years later, the culmination of our efforts with both Lynne and her co-author, Liz Andrews, has resulted in this book, which we have called *The Social Baby*.

The Social Baby is an example of how the studies of academics, 'hands-on' professionals and parents can come together to make information available for all in a palatable form. From the outset we were highly aware of how invasive getting images for the book might be – especially for first-time parents who may be feeling vulnerable and anxious following the birth. We owe an enormous debt of gratitude to the many families who allowed us to come into their homes to record the activities of their babies. To observe the best we had to be as 'invisible' as possible, so traditional flash photography was not an option. We used a discreet video camcorder to capture the intimate, sensitive and subtle moments of communication you will find in this book. These recordings were copied onto computer and 'imaged grabbed' for inclusion in the book. For the most part the filming took place within the families' homes in widely differing and often far from ideal light conditions. What some of the images may lack in quality is more than compensated for by what they reveal about infant behaviour. To our knowledge this collection of images is unprecedented, as is the presentation of the information contained in this remarkable book.

The production of *The Social Baby* has changed our lives forever, and the way we perceive new babies. We only wish we had had the knowledge we now have when our daughter was born, but as Lynne and Liz have said to us many times, Donald Winnicott coined the phrase *'the good enough parent'*. Nobody sets out to be anything less than the best parent they can and we hope this book will support and encourage everyone involved with babies, not just parents, to enjoy and understand the uniqueness of each baby.

Special thanks to Julie, John and their family for the privilege of letting us be present at the birth of Ethan; also to Liz, Bill, Stefanie and Max for their permission to use their personal video footage, and to all the other parents and babies who gave up their time and endured the inconvenience of us turning up to film at a time when they probably could have done without it!

Helen and Clive Dorman

Directors, The Children's Project

PREFACE

Our work over the past 25 years or so has been concerned with the development of infants. For one of us this has been largely the academic experience of a research psychologist concerned to understand the nature of infant development and the factors influencing its course. This has involved listening to many parents' accounts of their experience of caring for their baby in the early months, as well as carrying out observational and experimental studies of infants. For the other of us, this experience has been exclusively clinical work with parents and their young children, as a Health Visitor and counsellor.

Recently, with colleagues at the Winnicott Research Unit of the University of Reading and in the West Berkshire Health Trust, we have come together to develop a programme of care in pregnancy and the early postnatal months that is based on the research evidence. The focus of this programme is to help parents appreciate their baby's early capacities, especially their social responses. In addition, it is designed to help parents manage common areas of concern, such as their baby's crying or sleeping difficulties. This book is based on this care programme. Its purpose is to make available to parents information on aspects of infant development which will be both of interest to them and of help to them in the care of their baby in the first few months. The premise is that a deeper understanding of the baby's experience will increase the enjoyment of parenthood and child care.

Of course, mothers and fathers of young children are commonly in close touch with their primary care teams – their General Practitioner or their Health Visitor – and it is right that they should turn to these professionals for help with any difficulties they might be experiencing in caring for their baby. However, we know that many parents do not seek professional help for such problems and struggle on unsupported. We hope that for these parents this book may contain information which will be of use to them, or, where appropriate, encourage them to seek professional help. We also hope that, for parents who are lucky enough to have a baby who seldom cries, sleeps through the night and appears to find life nothing but a source of pleasure, this book will contain information about aspects of their baby's development which will enable them to have an even richer appreciation of their baby.

Lynne Murray, Liz Andrews

FOREWORD

Dr Donald Winnicott's broadcast talks on child rearing in the 1940's gave a new generation of women the freedom to follow their own instincts in the care of their infants, with so-called experts relegated to advising on essentially medical matters. 'But what do I do,' one woman asked Winnicott's disciple, Sir Peter Tizard, 'if I have three university degrees and no instincts?', while another said to me: 'If I was capable of taking all the advice handed out to me, I wouldn't have needed it'.

Lynne Murray, a professor of psychology and a Director of the Winnicott Research Unit based in Reading University, has now picked up the baton, using all the new knowledge about babies that has accumulated in the past half-century and to which she has been a distinguished contributor. If science is the systematic elaboration of the implications of directed observation, Professor Murray's work could be described as the science of what comes naturally. The chapter and verse for this science is provided by an engaging series of photographs of the baby's world before and after birth that illustrate her text. Her book, put together with Liz Andrews, a Health Visitor, is written for all who are interested in babies, especially their parents, and is eminently readable both as regards vocabulary and tone of voice. That they are both mothers themselves ensures that what the authors say has been tested in the real world of the nursery as well as in the laboratory.

One would hope that parents preparing for a new entrant to their family, especially their first child, will find in this book what they are looking for in the way of a guide to the pleasures and responsibility of parenthood in the first weeks and months after birth, based on their own recognition that a new-born child is from the start a person, albeit an immature one, rather than a bundle of physiological needs and reactions. As our population gets increasingly alienated from the traditional wisdom on baby care handed down from mother to daughter by example rather than instruction, it is very important for the future well-being of the nation (including those who are childless but will depend for their pensions on the work of other people's offspring) that, with a diminishing birth rate, we do our best to ensure that our child-rearing practices really do meet the complex emotional needs of the absolute beginners represented by the new-born. This may require a very considerable adjustment of social priorities on the part of government as well as individual families. We cannot afford to indulge in the momentous act of creating a new human being in the way that so many pet owners unreflectingly take on responsibilities that they cannot live up to. Parents know this and deserve support such as this book provides. Let us hope that it is also read by civil servants, politicians and members of those professions whom the public consult when they are worried about how they are coping with what is in many ways the most fundamental and important of our biologically driven activities.

John A Davis
Emeritus Professor of Paediatrics
University of Cambridge

March 2000

ACKNOWLEDGEMENTS

This book derives only in part from the experience of the authors. It owes a great deal to the work of numerous researchers and clinicians in the field of infant development who have so advanced our understanding of infancy and parenthood. Those whose ideas have played a particularly important part in our thinking are Donald Winnicott and his colleagues, Martin James and Madeleine Davis, as well as Colwyn Trevarthen and Berry Brazelton. More directly, we thank Pauline Dowding for helping us liaise with parents and their infants; David Andrews, Lindsay Cox and Melanie Gunning for their help in recording foetal behaviour; Jackie Peters and Liz Schofield for their assistance with recording infant responses to maternal odour; Janne Karpf and Claire Lawson for their help with recording parent-infant interactions, and Donna Webb for her assistance with the preparation of the text. We also thank Ian St James Roberts for his comments on infant crying, Peter Fleming and Dieter Wolke for their comments on sleeping, Wilf Stevenson for his comments on policies to support parents, and especially John Davis, Sheelah Seeley and Peter Cooper for their invaluable suggestions and comments on all aspects of the text, and James Sainsbury for his personal support.

We are also enormously grateful to all the families who allowed us to film them and their babies.

Finally, we are deeply indebted to Clive and Helen Dorman, whose talent and flair in photography and design have so enriched the communication of our ideas.

NOTE ON THE TEXT

Throughout this book, we have referred to the baby as 'she' in order to avoid the use of the more clumsy 'he/she'. However, all the information and advice in the book applies, of course, equally to boys.

PICTURE CREDITS

The publishers would like to thank the following for their kind permission to reproduce the images in this book:
16, 38 top, 38 bottom, 40, 41, 46 middle, 52, 53, 54, 55, 64, 65, 84 top, 84 bottom, 94 top, 118 top, 122-123 top picture story, 154 top, 166 top, Lynne Murray and Peter Cooper
17, David Andrews
36, 37, 97, Liz and Bill Walker
all other images Helen and Clive Dorman

INTRODUCTION

A hundred years ago the eminent psychologist, William James, considered the mental life of the baby to be a 'booming, buzzing confusion'. But in recent times our knowledge about babies' experience has grown enormously. Research has shown that, right from the start, babies have complex psychological lives. What might seem, on the surface, random and confused behaviour is, in fact, highly organised. Most dramatic among the baby's abilities, even in the first weeks of life, are their social responses. This ability is, of course, highly adaptive, since babies are totally dependent on others to care for them, and it is essential for their survival that they are in relationships that are reliable and sensitive to their needs. The fact that babies are so responsive to other people, and so expressive in their facial movements and gestures, even in the first few weeks of life, helps parents to give them the sensitive care that they need. By watching the subtle, changing pattern of a baby's expressions and movements, and by appreciating the significance of these cues, parents can become aware of the richness of the baby's experience, and can be guided to help their baby.

BABIES ARE INDIVIDUALS

As anyone who has had more than one baby will know (and even those with identical twins!), there are strong individual differences in the way babies behave right from the start. These arise for a whole host of reasons: for example, being born prematurely, or being relatively small, will have an effect on the baby's behaviour. But even babies who are born full term and who are of normal birth weight are very different from one another, although the basis for this variability is still poorly understood. Each baby has a unique set of genes, and even the environment in the womb is very variable. Differences such as the baby being particularly sensitive to changes in her environment early on, or being able to sleep through a party going on in the same room – can have a profound impact on the people who are caring for her. Yet much of the information and advice available to new parents ignores this variability, giving only a general description of a 'normal' baby, particularly in the areas of sleeping and crying. These are commonly areas of concern to parents, and it can be distressing when your own baby just doesn't seem to behave in the manner described in the books and pamphlets. Statements such as 'babies usually begin to sleep through the night by so many weeks, months', although true in general, can feel undermining if your baby doesn't behave as is suggested. The casual questions of well-meaning professionals or relatives, if they assume a 'normal' baby, can also be felt as a challenge: 'Is he smiling yet?' can be interpreted as: 'He should be smiling by now, and if he's not, then something's wrong'.

A central theme of this book is that by watching your own baby – understanding that your baby's behaviour is not random but can tell you something important about how the baby is experiencing the world – you can be guided to give the care that is most appropriate. General descriptions of the development of babies *are* given in this book, but their purpose is to help parents appreciate the baby's early capabilities, rather than to set out what 'ought' to happen at any given time. It is important for parents to realise that babies will vary a great deal in how these capabilities are shown and develop.

CHAPTER ONE

THE BABY'S SOCIAL WORLD

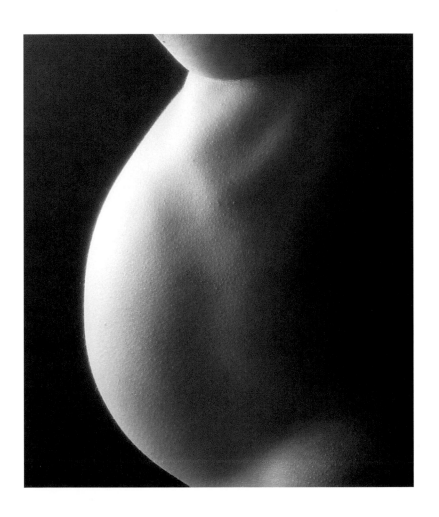

GETTING TO KNOW THE WORLD BEFORE BIRTH

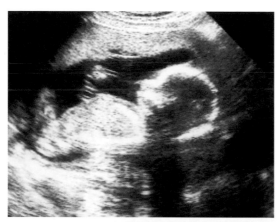

Even before birth, babies are part of a social world. Hearing the sound of the mother's voice, and those of the people around her, gives the unborn baby direct access to the social world into which she will emerge. The baby will also sense the rhythms of the mother's daily routine, the quiet and busy times. The mother's level of stress, her diet, whether or not she smokes, her cycles of activity, all become part of the unborn baby's experience.

1 One week to go before Jamie's brother, Alex, is born. Alex is moving around and kicking, and Jamie is keen to feel the movements himself.

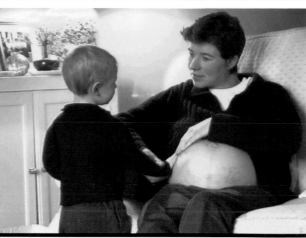

2 Catherine helps Jamie find the best place to feel Alex's foot moving.

3 Jamie rather shyly feels around, moving his hand gently, sharing the experience with his mother.

4 He leans forward to plant a kiss where his baby brother's kick can be felt.

5 Jamie strokes the baby and talks to him, the beginnings of their relationship already taking shape in Jamie's imagination.

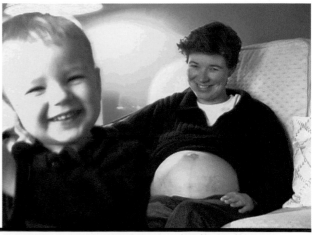

6 Jamie's excitement is mounting, but he is also apprehensive, and he makes sure he has his security blanket with him when he engages in these imaginary encounters.

Near the end of pregnancy, by around 36 weeks, the baby will usually have started to develop her own cycles of restful and active phases. Charts 1 and 2 right show how one baby's rhythms developed: the first is a record of the activity of a baby boy called Alex in the 28th week of pregnancy, when there is little sign of clear periods of quiet and active states. The second, taken at 34 weeks, shows that his behaviour is becoming more organised; he is quiet for the first 20 minutes, but then he becomes very lively! These movements can be felt clearly by Alex's mother, and even by the other members of the family when they place their hands on her abdomen.

At about the same stage of pregnancy, when the baby notices more about events going on close by, he also starts to control his responses to them. Chart 3 below shows how Alex responded to the sound of a buzzer, heard repeatedly over three minutes through the wall of the womb at 38 weeks. When Alex first hears it, he responds with a vigorous kick, and his heart rate goes up, but as it is repeated he gradually learns to 'switch off', and only small movements are seen on the chart. Even an event repeated for a few minutes just once or twice a day, such as hearing the theme tune of a soap opera that the mother watches regularly, can become an experience to which the unborn baby will respond as familiar!

1. 28 WEEKS' GESTATION

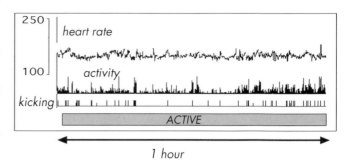

1 hour

2. 34 WEEKS' GESTATION

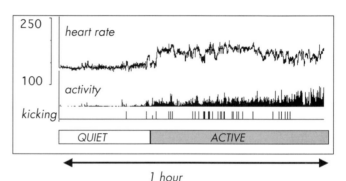

1 hour

3. FOETAL HABITUATION

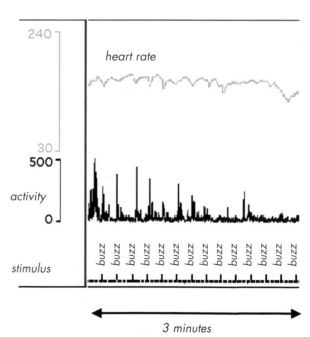

3 minutes

THE NEWBORN'S FIRST SOCIAL ENCOUNTERS
'Nice to meet you'

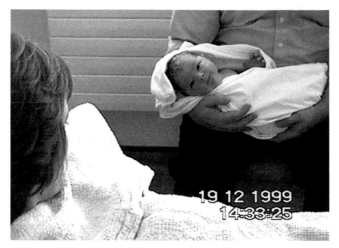

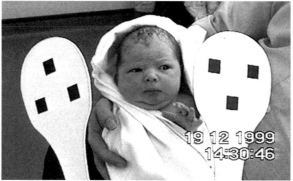

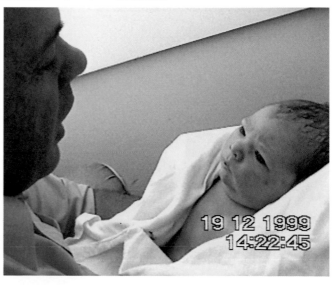

If the birth has been straightforward, and the baby has not received much maternal medication, immediately after the birth the baby is often wide awake, settled and calm, and intently interested in her surroundings for some hours before settling into a sleepy state. This alert period gives the baby and her parents a good opportunity to connect with each other. Within minutes of birth, the baby can show her preference for contact with people, rather than objects. For example, the baby will turn her head to the sound of someone's voice, when another sound, even if of the same pitch and intensity, will not attract her attention. The baby has already heard voices before she was born, so this response is partly based on her previous experience. But the baby is also attracted to faces, something she has certainly not come across before! Given a choice between looking at a face-shaped pattern, and one with the arrangement of eyes, nose and mouth scrambled up, the newborn baby will spend longer looking at the face.

One of the most dramatic abilities of the newborn that shows she is ready for social contacts with other people is her ability to imitate another person's facial expression. A baby just a few minutes old, if content and alert, will gaze intently at the face of another person, watching them seriously. If the adult clearly and slowly moves her own face, for example, opening her mouth wide, or protruding her tongue, the baby will watch intently and then imitate the adult expression. It is as if the baby can already sense that she and the other person are in some way the same.

Of course small babies have not had enough experience of the world to feel complex, self-conscious, emotions like shame, guilt or embarrassment. But apart from these emotions, the baby can show us that she is fully human from the start by the wide range of her emotional expressions, including disgust, sadness, joy, fear and interest.

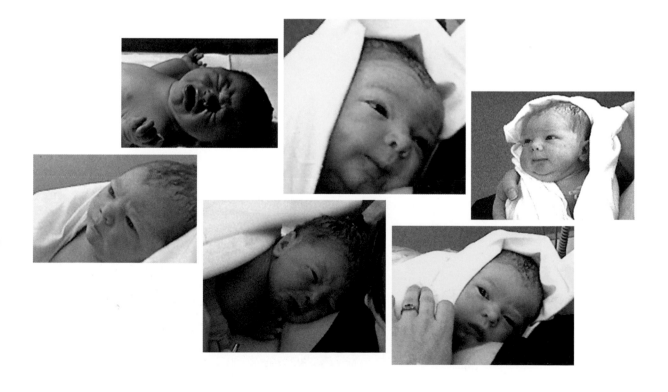

Picture story

ETHAN IS BORN *The time shown here is 14.07.55*

*Ethan has had a normal delivery. Weighing 4.281kg (9lbs 7oz),
he is a healthy baby, and immediately shows that he has the
ability to comfort himself by sucking on his thumb.*

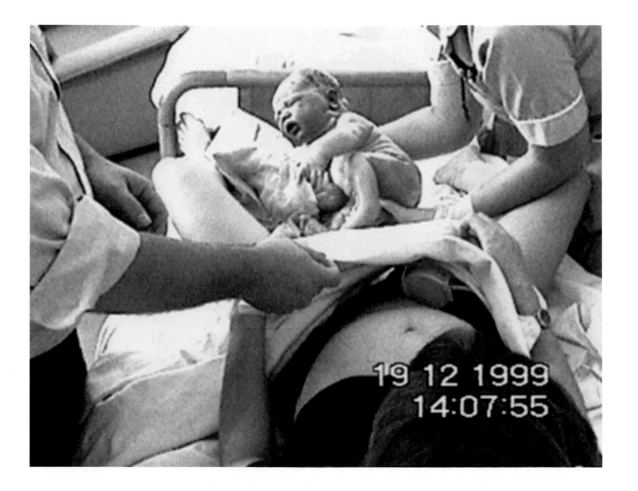

19 12 1999
14:07:55

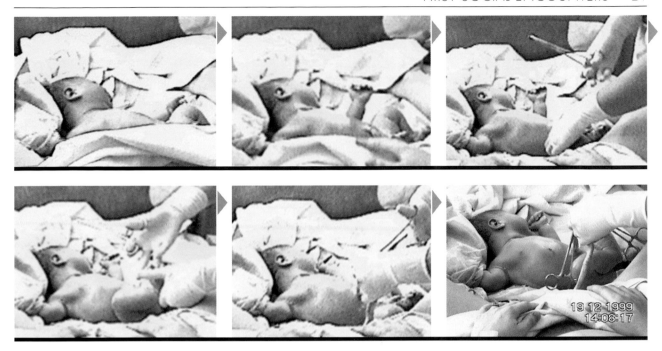

The midwife lays Ethan down so that she can cut the cord. Ethan brings his left hand up to his mouth and, not even half a minute old, he has found his thumb and sucks on it.

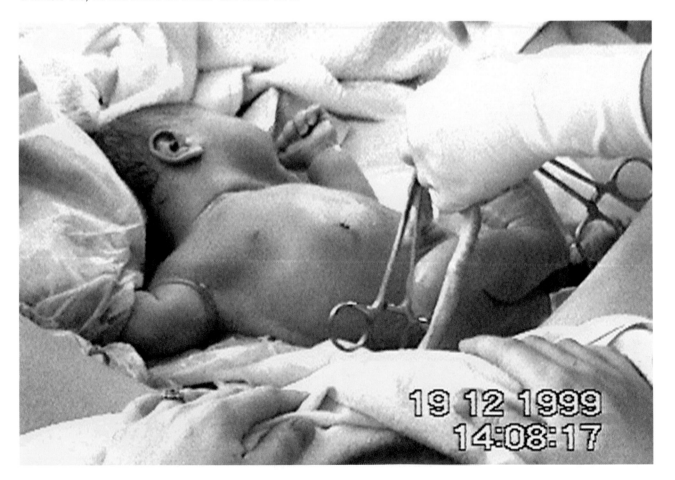

🎥 *Picture story*
THE FIRST MINUTE

Ethan's first experience of the world is not easy, as he is taken away from the delivery bed and has to experience being handled by the midwife.

Once returned to his mother, however, he is quickly calmed.

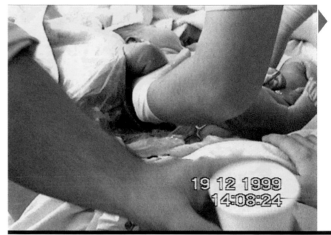

1 The midwife lifts Ethan and takes him away to check his breathing.

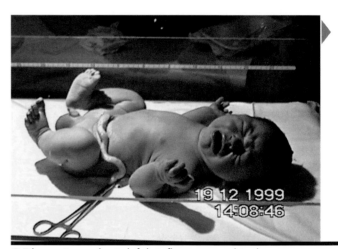

4 Ethan cries as he is left briefly uncovered in the cot, eyes tightly shut in the glare of the bright light.

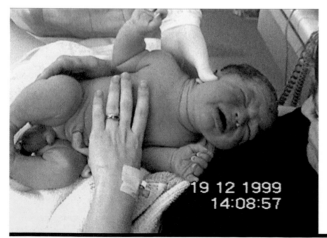

7 As he is placed on his mother, the thrashing of his arms is contained.

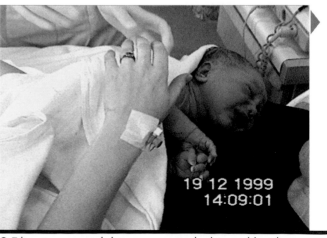

8 Ethan is wrapped, his arms are tucked in and his distress subsides.

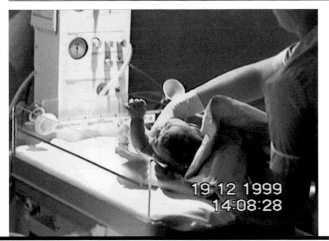

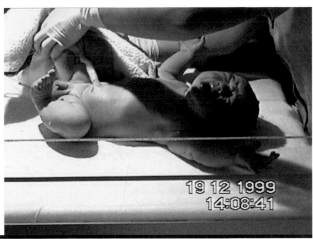

2 Ethan's arm jerks up as he is moved, and he loses his thumb, which he was sucking.

3 He flails around as the wraps are removed.

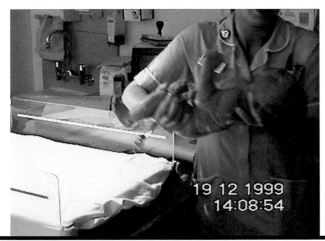

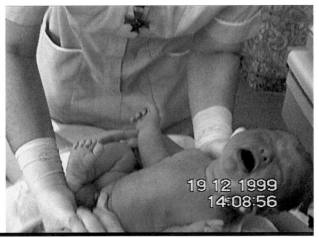

5 Having checked Ethan is breathing normally, the midwife can now take him back.

6 Ethan is still distressed as he is passed back to his mother.

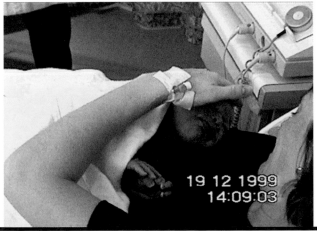

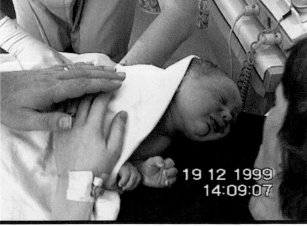

9 Ethan's mother strokes his head and greets him, and he becomes calm.

11 Just a minute since his birth, and Ethan is finally settled, looking comfortable and relaxed as he is held in his mother's arms.

📽 *Picture story*

ETHAN MEETS HIS MOTHER

Now Ethan is comfortable he can start to take in the world around him

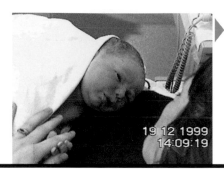

1 Ethan opens his eyes, and looks directly at his mother, Julie.

2

3

THERE ARE INTERRUPTIONS,

and Ethan has to cope with new events

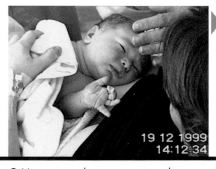

1 As Ethan continues to gaze at Julie, his father, John, starts to stroke Ethan's forehead.

2 The stroking interrupts Ethan's eye contact with his mother.

3 He starts to become agitated.

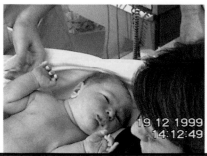
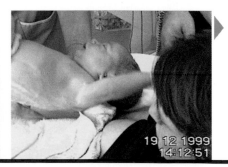

7 Now there is another interruption. Ethan's blanket is removed…

8 …and he startles.

9 His arms fly out as the midwife lifts him.

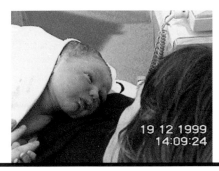

4 He watches her intently, his eyes scanning the details of her face.

5

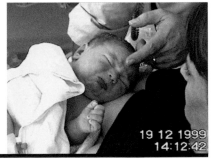

4 Ethan brings his thumb up to his mouth, but doesn't quite manage to suck. He screws up his eyes.

5 Ethan looks unhappy, and he grimaces as the stroking continues.

6

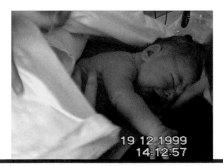

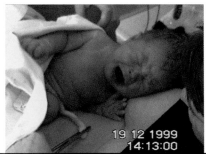

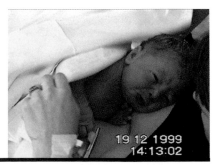

10 Ethan is still distressed as he is lowered back onto Julie's breast...

11 ...and the cord is clamped.

12 He looks back at his mother's face, still unhappy with all the disruption.

🎥 *Picture story*

ETHAN GETS TO KNOW HIS MOTHER

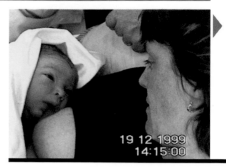

1 Soon Ethan and his mother are back in contact. The midwife has put Ethan to the breast, but in fact he's not interested in feeding; he wants only to look at Julie's face.

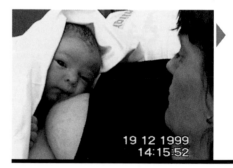

5 Occasionally Ethan looks around, as there are voices and movements nearby.

8 ...even making gentle cooing sounds.

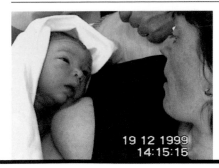

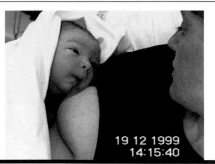

2 Ethan watches his mother intently again.

3 As Julie talks to him, Ethan's face becomes more mobile and expressive.

4

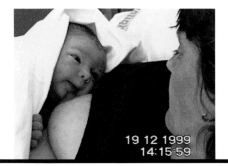

6 But he quickly resumes contact with his mother...

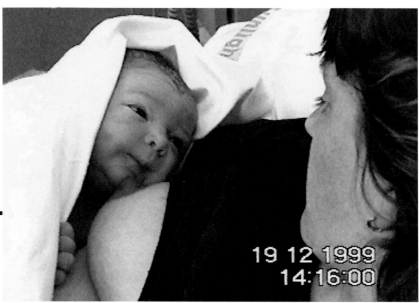

7 ...and appears to take real pleasure in engaging with her...

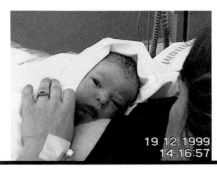

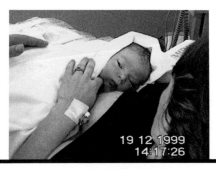

9 A little later Ethan notices his father's voice, as John talks to Julie.

10 Ethan turns to look at his father, his face stilling as he listens...

11 ...then he shifts his gaze back to Julie's face as she replies.

📽 *Picture story*

ETHAN GETS TO KNOW HIS FATHER

While the midwife is busy with Ethan's mother, Ethan has the opportunity to spend time with his father, John. Ethan explores John's face intently for a few minutes, scanning the length and breadth of his features. John then sets up a demonstration of Ethan's ability to imitate facial movements, clearly and slowly either protruding his tongue, or opening his mouth wide. On each occasion Ethan concentrates hard, and then imitates the appropriate action.

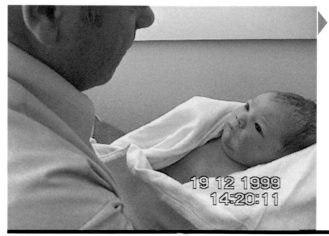

1 Ethan gazes intently at his father...

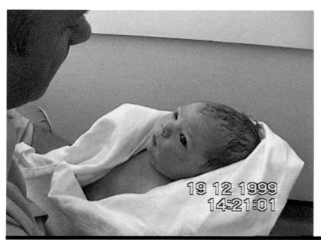

4 His eyes scan John's features...

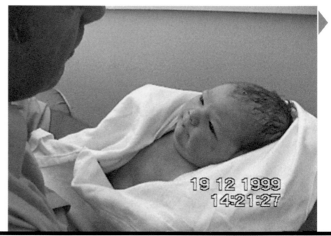

5

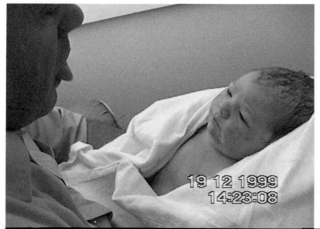

8 John slowly and clearly protrudes his tongue, and Ethan attends closely.

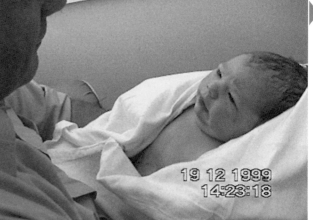

9 Ethan continues to look seriously at his father, and then he begins to move his mouth.

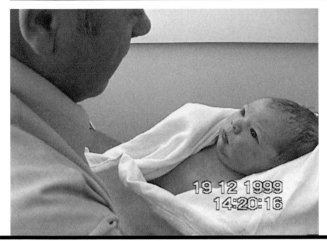

2 ...he is concentrated and serious...

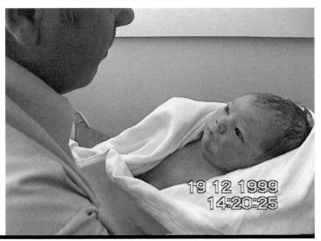

3 ...and thoroughly explores John's face.

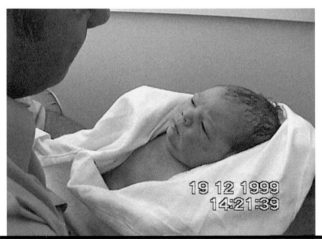

6 ...and he remains totally absorbed for some minutes.

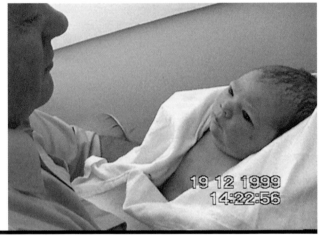

7

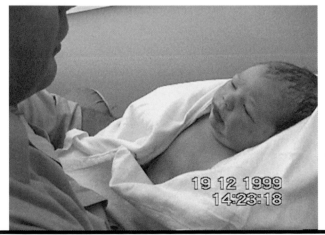

10 Ethan appears to be concentrating completely on his mouth as he frowns and shuts his eyes...

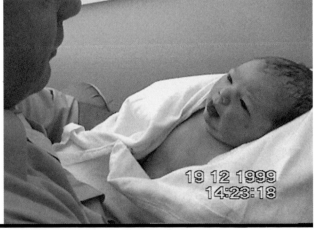

11 ...then he looks back at his father as he protrudes his own tongue.

continues on the next page

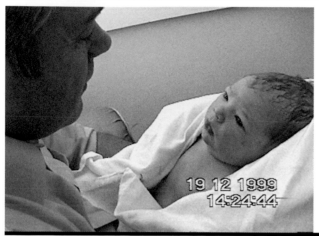

12 A little later, and Ethan is still watching his father.

continued from previous page

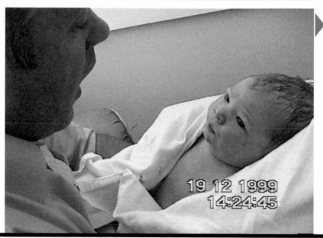

13 Now John opens his mouth wide, Ethan monitoring closely.

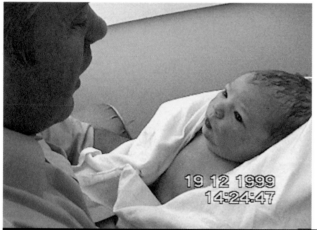

16 ...as his own lips approximate to the model his father has posed, Ethan looks back again...

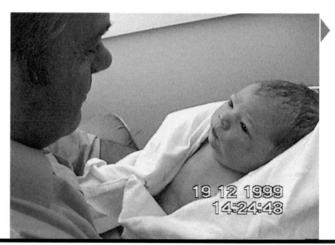

17 ...and then relaxes.

20 ...and once again he glances to one side...

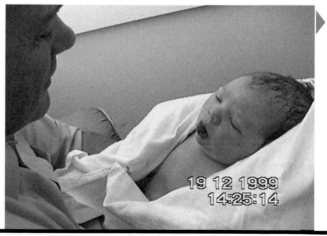

21 ...before closing his eyes as he produces his own version of his father's expression.

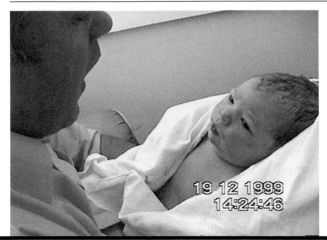

14 Ethan's gaze shifts away a fraction as his lips begin to purse...

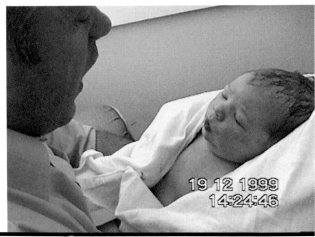

15 ...and he once again shuts his eyes as he seems to concentrate all his energy into moving his mouth...

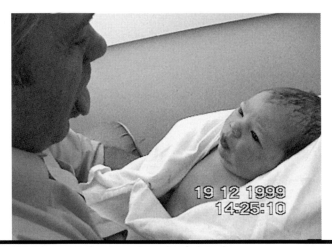

18 Ethan watches intently as his father demonstrates a final tongue protrusion.

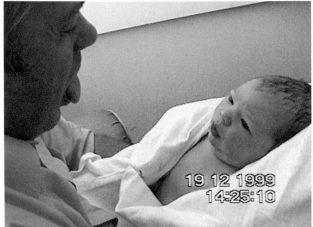

19 Ethan's mouth begins to move...

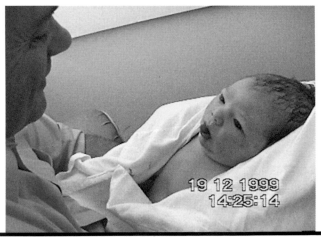

22 Ethan protrudes his own tongue clearly...

23 ...leaving his father proud and delighted.

📽 *Picture story*

ETHAN PREFERS TO LOOK AT THE FACE-LIKE PATTERN

Two paddle boards are held up for Ethan, at just the right distance for him to focus on them. One board has simple black shapes set out in a face-like pattern, whereas on the other, the pattern is upside down.

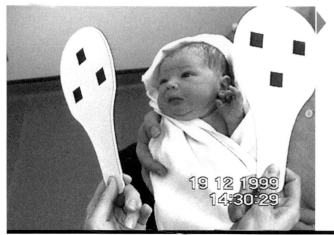

1 Ethan's attention is initially caught by the upside-down pattern.

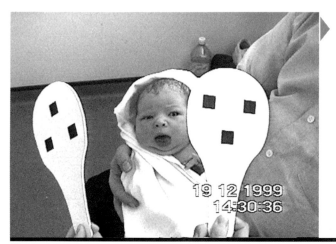

4

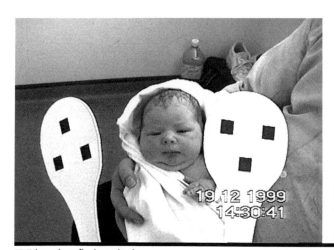

7 Ethan briefly breaks his gaze...

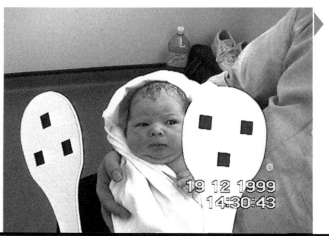

8 ...but then he quickly resumes looking at the face-like pattern...

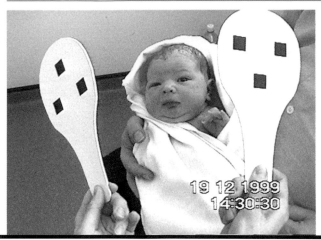

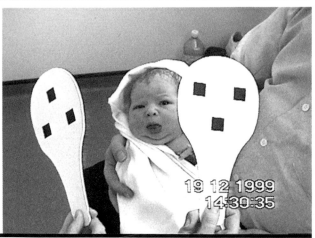

2 But he quickly turns away and his eyes scan across to the face-like form.

3 The face pattern really holds Ethan's attention and he looks at the board intently.

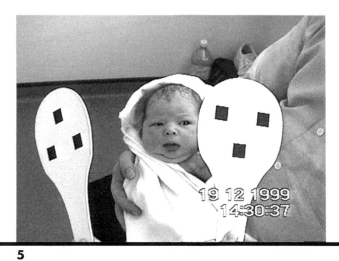

5

6

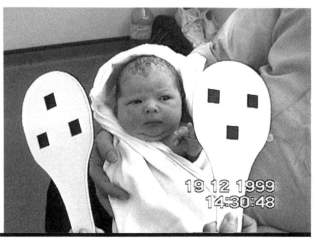

9 ...ignoring the other paddle board.

10

Picture story

ETHAN TURNS TO THE SOUND OF HIS MOTHER'S VOICE

Still on the labour ward, Ethan's mother is having a rest, while John sits close beside her, holding Ethan.

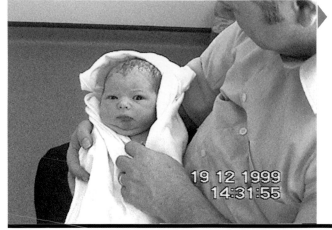

1 Ethan is calm and alert as he lies in his father's arms.

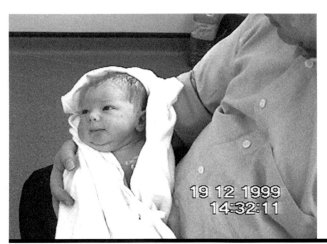

4

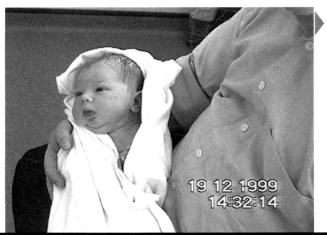

5

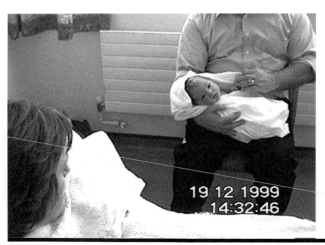

8

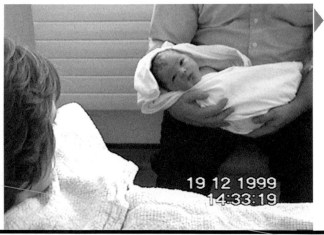

9 As Julie continues to talk to Ethan, he becomes more active, and his face becomes more mobile and expressive.

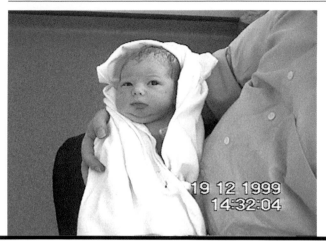

2 John raises his head to speak to Julie, and Ethan looks up.

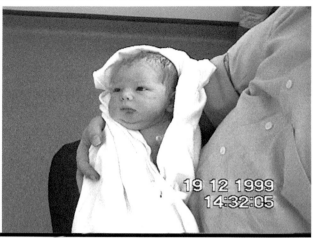

3 As Julie replies, Ethan turns his head, and he starts to become more animated.

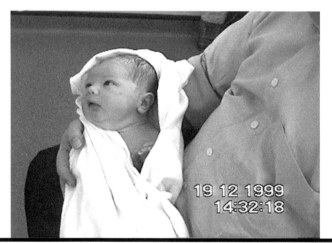

6 Julie now calls Ethan, and he turns more actively towards her.

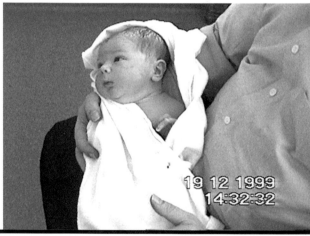

7 Although Julie is too far away for Ethan to be able to see her clearly, he is strongly drawn to respond to her voice.

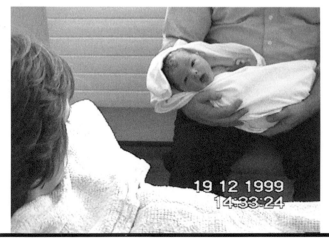

10

11 It gives Julie the powerful feeling that her newborn son is really engaged in communicating with her.

📽 *Picture story*

THE EXPERIENCES OF A PREMATURELY BORN BABY AND HIS PARENTS

Max, 3 days – 7 weeks

Not all babies have a straightforward start in life: they can be born prematurely, for example, or the baby's growth may not have progressed well. The medical interventions that these kinds of problem necessitate, as well as the baby's own state of health, can make the development of the baby's relationships with her family more complicated in the early weeks, and possibly months. Nevertheless, even in such difficult circumstances, a baby's expressiveness, and her powerful impulse to make connections with those who are caring for her, can help to fuel parents' and siblings' sense of being in contact with her.

Max was born 12 weeks before term, at 28 weeks' gestation. He was, however, a healthy baby, being a good weight for his age (1.36kg [3lbs] at birth), and able to breathe on his own. For the first few days he needed to be drip-fed and, as it was hard for him to suck, he was then fed on his mother's expressed breast milk through tubes via his nose or mouth. By the time he was three weeks old, however, he was able to start breast-feeding, and by seven weeks he was fully breast-fed. When he was eight weeks old, he went home.

1 Max is three days old. His mother, Liz, and sister Stefanie observe him through the walls of his special cot.

5 Max is now three weeks old, and he looks far more robust. He is no longer drip-fed, and although he receives most of his mother's expressed milk by a tube via his nose, he is starting to breast-feed.

9 ...and opens it wide as he continues to watch his father's face...

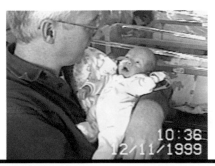

10 ...Bill feels as though Max is really communicating as he continues this activity, and looks so alert and interested.

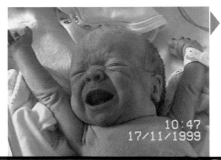

11 One week later (and five weeks before his due date of birth), Max no longer needs to be fed through tubes. He cries vigorously.

2 Here, Max is drip-fed and kept warm, and he receives treatment for mild jaundice. Handling him in his cot is done through 'portholes'.

3 As Max is able to breathe on his own and is generally healthy, he can be taken from his cot. Liz supports Stefanie as she reaches out to her baby brother. To Stefanie's great delight, Max's hand curls around her finger.

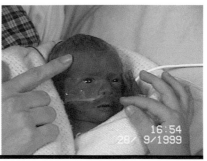

4 Liz and Stefanie are not quite sure whether Max can see anything clearly, but they certainly have the powerful impression that he is really looking at Stefanie's face.

6 Holding Max feels quite comfortable, now that he is developing so well.

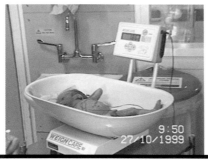

7 A weigh-in at four weeks shows that Max has put on half a kilogram since birth – good progress.

8 Max is six weeks old. His father, Bill, is holding him. Max looks at his father and shapes his mouth...

12 Liz lifts him from the cot...

13 ...and brings Max up to her shoulder.

14 Max moulds in to his mother, and is quickly calmed and soothed by the security her contact provides.

THE START OF SPECIAL RELATIONSHIPS

'This is someone I know'

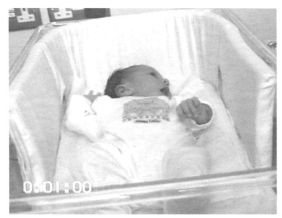

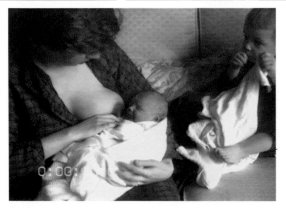

From birth babies show a general preference for people rather than objects. But they also quickly begin to notice the particular qualities of the people who are caring for them. It is as if the baby is ready to form special relationships with those who will make up her close social world, and on whom she will depend. Even before birth, the baby picks up some of the characteristics of her mother – the taste of amniotic fluid, for example, gives the baby information about the taste of her mother's milk and her odour. Within the first hours after birth she will show that she prefers her own mother's odour to that of another mother by turning towards a pad her mother has been wearing rather than one worn by another woman. In the same way, before birth, the baby has picked up some of the qualities of her mother's voice, and she will respond to her mother talking to her in preference to anyone else. Although the baby has obviously not been able to gain information about her mother's appearance before birth, she is very ready to learn about it, and within just a day or so she will spend longer looking at her mother's face than at the face of another woman.

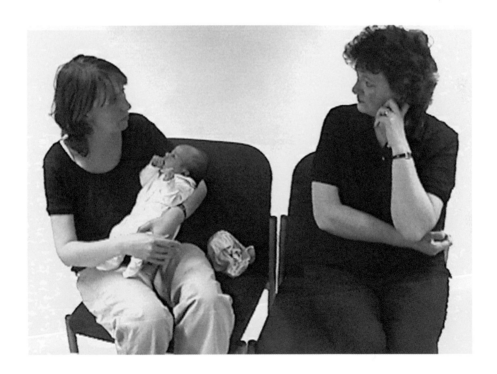

📽 *Picture story*

ODOUR TEST IN THE RESEARCH UNIT

Alexandra H, 2 weeks

In this experiment the baby lies in a specially designed cot. A box is secured on each side of her head, each containing a soft tissue pad. One of them is impregnated with her own mother's odour, and the other with the odour of another woman who has a baby of the same age. Fans blow air through the pads on each side so that their odour wafts into the cot. For the first minute of the experiment the baby's own mother's pad is in the box on the baby's right-hand side. Then the pads are changed over, so that for the next minute her mother's pad is on her left. The amount of time the baby spends turned to either one side or the other is used to estimate the strength of her preference for her mother's odour. In this experiment, Alexandra, who is 13 days old, spends 73% of the two one-minute periods turned towards her own mother's pad, well above the threshold taken as an indication of preference.

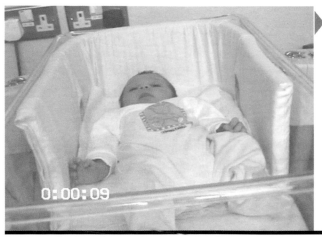

1 Alexandra lies alert and contented in the cot as the fans on each side of her head start up. She is perfectly still for the first few seconds.

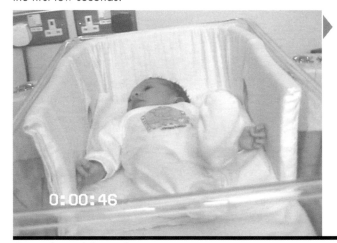

4 ...right until the end...

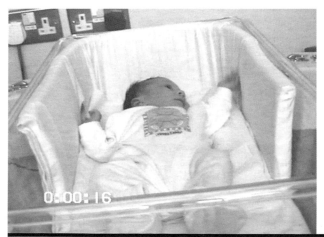

7 Soon, however, she makes her choice, and turns to the new location for her mother's odour, and she stays oriented to her left...

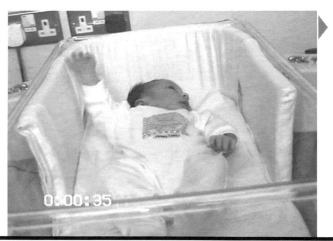

8 ...for almost all of the remaining time.

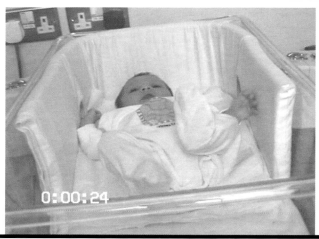

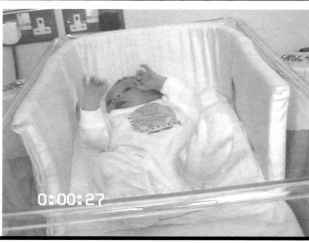

2 After a while Alexandra starts to become active, but she has still not turned to one side or the other.

3 Now she turns to her right, where her own mother's pad is secured. She remains in this position…

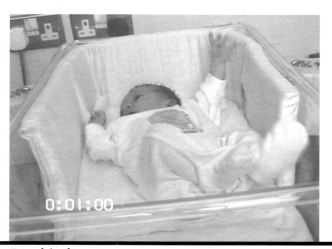

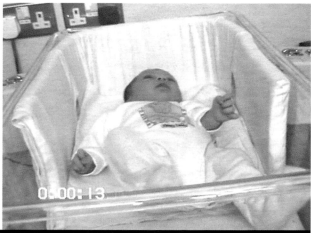

5 …of the first minute.

6 The pads have been changed over, so Alexandra's mother's pad is now on her left. Once again, for the first few seconds, she does not turn.

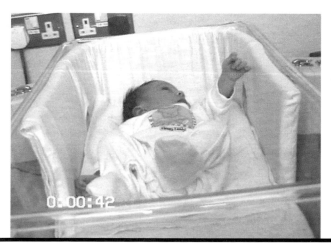

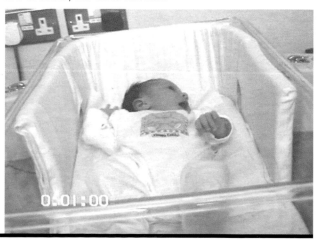

9 Alexandra moves her arms and legs excitedly…

10 …and makes mouthing movements as she faces the source of her mother's odour.

📽 *Picture story*

THE BABY'S RESPONSE TO HER MOTHER AND A STRANGER

Emily D, 5 weeks

Liz is a Research Health Visitor who has handled Emily before and they have had an enjoyable time. Nevertheless, Emily is not entirely comfortable in Liz's relatively unfamiliar arms. When her mother holds her, by contrast, Emily snuggles in and moulds to her.

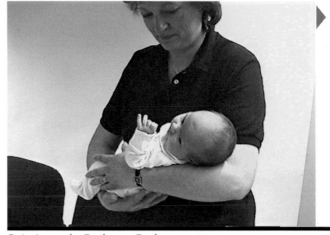

1 As Liz picks Emily up, Emily turns away...

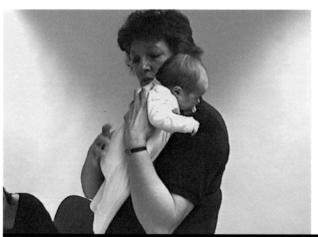

4 Liz tries lifting Emily up to her shoulder, but Emily remains tense and stiff.

5 Emily tolerates Liz rocking her, but she keeps her distance.

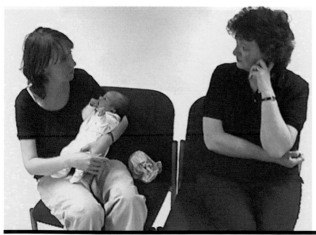

8 She sucks on her fist, keeping a close eye on her mother, and nestling in to her.

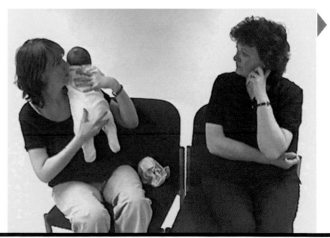

9 Siobhan lifts Emily up onto her shoulder.

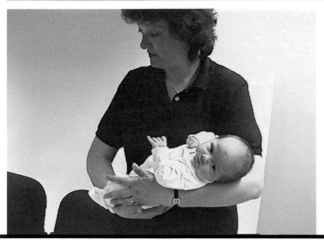

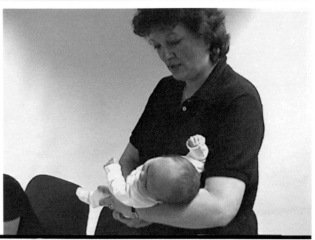

2 ...keeping her mother, Siobhan, in view...

3 ...and resisting Liz's attempts to draw her in.

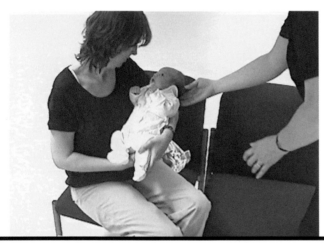

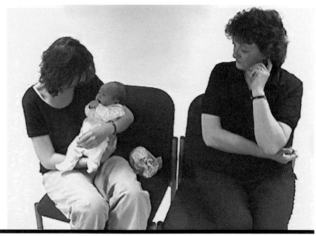

6 Liz passes Emily back to Siobhan, and Emily gazes intently at her mother's face.

7 Emily relaxes and looks more comfortable – there is no turning out and away from her mother's familiar arms.

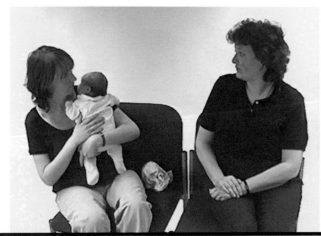

10 Emily turns towards her mother, trying to get as close as possible to her.

11 She snuggles in, and buries her face in her mother's neck.

Picture story

INDIVIDUAL DIFFERENCES IN RESPONSES TO CUDDLING

Emily R, 7 weeks

Although the response to being held by a parent can differ in obvious ways from that shown towards a stranger, with snuggling or nestling-in occurring preferentially with family members, it is not always the case that a baby will seek close physical contact with the people who look after her. Indeed, one dimension of striking individual differences between babies in the early weeks that can have a considerable impact on the parent's experience and feelings, is the way in which the baby responds to being held and cuddled.

Some babies just do not relax or mould into the parents' arms, but will resist and pull away. If the parent believes this is a personal response to them, or feels that it reflects their handling of the baby, such behaviour can be demoralising, and they may feel rejected. There is, however, no evidence to suggest that the parents' handling of the baby is the cause of this kind of response: it is simply one of the ways babies differ from one another early on. In such cases, it can be helpful to a parent to be aware of other kinds of cues, or signals from the baby, such as her gaze or other facial expressions, that may be observed when she is not in such close proximity to the parent, and that show her preferential responsiveness to them.

1 Emily is perfectly happy and contented, but she does not snuggle into her mother, Colette, as she holds her...

5 As Emily is lifted up, her posture is stiff and unyielding, and her head is kept tilted back.

6 It is hard for Colette to make eye contact with Emily when Emily adopts this position.

2 ...and Emily keeps her head tilted away.

3 Emily begins to twist further away from her mother...

4 ...but she remains calm and contented.

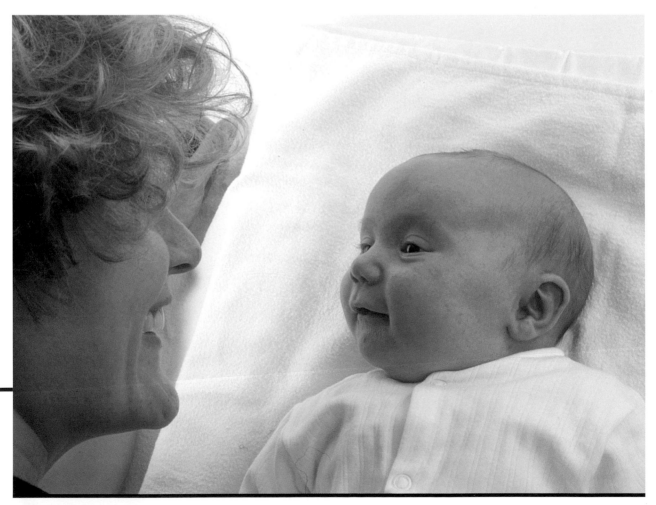

7 Once Emily is no longer held, but is securely propped against a cushion, she is delighted to engage face-to-face with Colette, and their intimacy is evident in their mutual gaze and smiles.

COMMUNICATION WITH PEOPLE
'Let's chat'

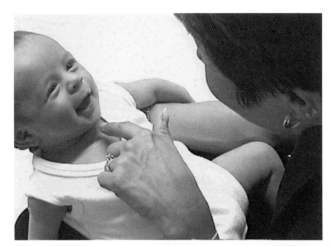

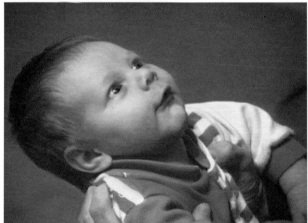

Babies are attracted to other people from birth and they quickly prefer the people who have become familiar. But the baby doesn't simply want to be near her family and their friends – she wants to share her experience with other people and interact with them!

Over the first few weeks the baby gradually becomes more active in her social contacts. She can be helped to enjoy 'chatting' with her social partners. In the first three months, the best distance for the baby to see someone's face in focus is 22cm (9in), and it helps in the early weeks if the baby's head is well supported. Some babies find it more difficult than others to hold their head up, and they will need support for some time. This is particularly likely with babies who were born prematurely. Being aware of the baby's state is also important: if the baby is sleepy, hungry, or in pain, the last thing she will feel like is being sociable. If, however, the baby is contented and alert, and in a comfortable position, she is likely to be keen to interact.

In the first weeks, the baby's active involvement in face-to-face communication is often rather fleeting, so, although she is very interested in other people, having prolonged 'conversations' is unusual. As the weeks go by, however, the baby will be able to remain interested for longer periods; eye-to-eye contact can be sustained, smiling becomes more reliable, and the baby can begin to play a more active role in interactions.

On such occasions the baby's mouth is often very mobile, with her tongue coming forward out of her mouth, or pushing into her lower lip, or she may open her mouth wide. These bursts of active effort can last for a number of seconds. It seems as though the baby is trying to talk and, indeed, some scientists have called this behaviour 'pre-speech' because, although not often accompanied by sound in the first weeks, it seems to serve the role of speech, reflecting the baby's efforts to communicate. Even the baby's limb movements can form a part of the baby's social behaviour, her arms rising, and her fingers often opening and pointing in concert when her mouthing reaches its peak. At such times, parents often make remarks such as 'That's a good story you're telling me', sensing that the baby's behaviour reflects her impulse to be sociable. When the partner picks up on the baby's cues and responds, this sustains the baby's involvement, and prolonged, two-way 'conversations' can take place in which the baby and her partner take turns watching and then being active in the dialogue.

📽 *Picture story*

THE NEED FOR HEAD SUPPORT

*Max, 11 weeks
(1 week before his due date
of delivery)*

*Babies vary in how easily
they are able to hold up their
heads. Max finds this quite
difficult in the first few weeks.
Although he is very sociable,
and would like to engage in
face-to-face play, when seated
upright it is hard for him to
control his head and maintain
eye contact. Tilting his chair
securely so that his head is
well supported makes a big
difference.*

1 Max is wide-eyed, eager to play.

2 He makes active gestures and mouth movements.

4 ...and in a moment he has lost control and he slumps.

5 Max frowns and becomes agitated...

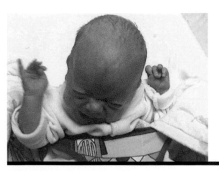

7 ...and he appears frustrated and distressed.

8 As his chair is tilted back, Max's head receives better support...

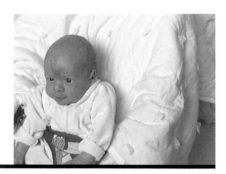

3 When his mother responds, Max watches contentedly, but his head is beginning to drop...

6 ...he tries to lift his head to make eye contact, but it is just too heavy for him...

9 ...and he once again enjoys some social play.

The kind of contacts that babies most enjoy in the first few weeks are those that follow the baby's own behaviour and expressions. Parents intuitively find themselves imitating the baby, often doing so very clearly and in a slightly emphasised way, possibly using their voice and whole face to mirror back, for example, the baby opening her mouth – this gives the baby clear and enriched feedback of her own action. The emotional quality of the partner's response also tends to match the general quality of the baby's behaviour, frowning when the baby frowns, showing pleasure when the baby looks content. This kind of 'mirroring' responsiveness is particularly effective in sustaining the baby's attention and involvement. The paediatrician, Donald Winnicott, believed that mirroring the baby's experience has the important function of helping the baby to establish a 'sense of self'; he believed that the experience of having her own actions and feelings reflected back in the behaviour of someone else affirms, enriches, and gives greater coherence to the baby's original experience.

The timing of the partner's responses is also something that the baby will notice: if the partner's feedback is sensitively paced, a response coming within a short time of the baby's, the baby is likely to continue watching her partner. If the response is delayed by some seconds, the baby may lose interest, as though she no longer has the sense that the other person's behaviour is linked to her own. Similarly, if the person interacting with the baby responds before the baby is ready, or is very swift and abrupt in their movements, this can interfere with the baby's engagement and lead to her attention switching elsewhere. This does not mean that parents should feel under pressure to be 'perfect' conversational partners for the baby, behaving like machines that are invariably accurate. For, while extreme disruptions do indeed distress the baby, the ordinary, small deviations that are quickly corrected, and that are a normal part of natural conversation, give the baby opportunities to experience how contacts are regained.

At times, the baby can become highly aroused and excited during these 'conversations', and may even seem to be overloaded with the intensity of the interaction. At such points, she may break off and turn her gaze away, before calming and making eye contact again in readiness for more social play. Subtle signs that the baby may be tiring and want a break from the stimulation of social play include changes in facial expression, like frowns and grimaces, yawns, and even possetting (see p.108). There can also be more obvious signs of cutting off, such as becoming self-absorbed, or arching her back and turning away. Respecting the baby's need to take time out, or her waning interest in 'conversation', will help prevent the baby becoming agitated or even distressed.

📽 *Picture story*

THE BABY'S ACTIVE COMMUNICATION 1

Natasha, 3 weeks

Natasha is only three weeks old, and her use of facial expression, mouthing and tongue movements for communication is still rather limited. Nevertheless, she watches her mother's face with fascination, and her interest and enthusiasm are also apparent in her hand and arm movements, as she reaches and gestures towards her mother.

1

THE BABY'S ACTIVE COMMUNICATION 2

Zak, 5 weeks

When alert and content, with head well supported, babies of just a few weeks old often appear keen to participate in what look like 'conversations' with a sympathetic partner. The baby communicates with a rich range of facial expressions, tongue movements and active shapings of the mouth that are often accompanied by hand and arm gestures. This kind of activity, although not often vocal in the first weeks, has been termed 'pre-speech',* since it seems to serve the same function as speech in adult conversation – and indeed, parents will often make comments such as 'You've got a lot to tell me today', that support this interpretation.

1

Here, we see Zak totally absorbed in communication with Liz. Initially, he watches her intently, but quickly begins to take an active role. He shapes his mouth in different positions, and his tongue is very mobile, moving inside his mouth, but also protruding beyond his lips. At times, as he raises his arms, he will extend his index finger at the peak of the arm movement, as if making a particularly important point! Long before words emerge, essential elements of human engagement are in place.

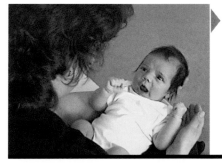

5

*The term 'pre-speech' was coined by Colwyn Trevarthen.

9

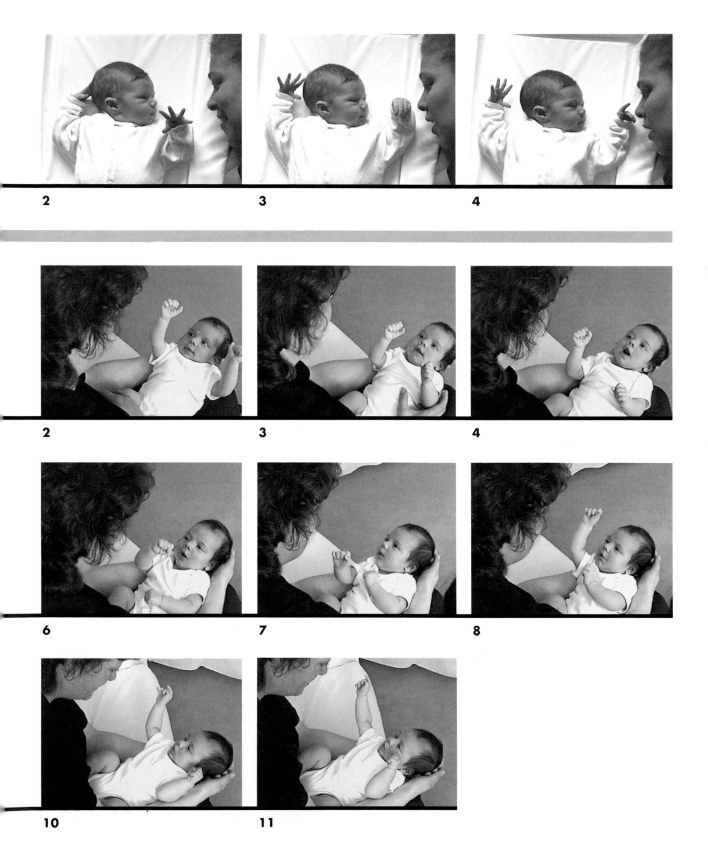

2   **3**   **4**

2   **3**   **4**

6   **7**   **8**

10   **11**

📽 *Picture story*

MIRRORING

William, 8 weeks

Face-to-face play with babies in the second and third months can seem like a musical duet, with distinct phrases when the baby's initiative is taken up by the parent who, quite unconsciously, mirrors, builds on and develops the baby's original communication. Play is intimate, and concerns nothing but the feelings and expressions of the two partners. The parents' mirroring is a very immediate way of conveying their acceptance of the baby, and it can both affirm and enrich the baby's experience.

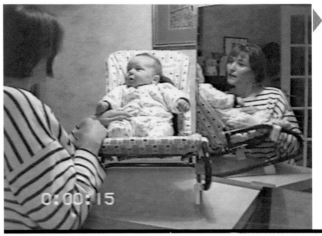

1 Helen, William's mother, listens attentively as William gestures and 'talks' to her.

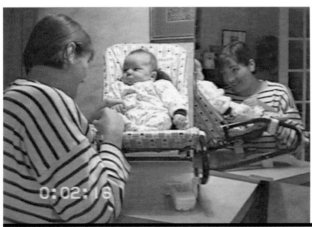

4 Another conversational phrase is about to begin, as Helen encourages William to play.

5 William actively mouths and gestures widely, and Helen tracks his changing expression…

8 William has started to make 'pre-speech' tonguing movements, to which Helen gives her full attention.

9 William's communication becomes more actively expressive, and Helen's mood shifts in response.

(To take these pictures with just one camera, we placed a mirror next to William.)

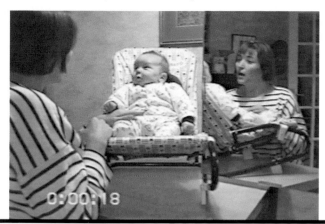

2 She shows that she takes what he is saying very seriously.

3 When William becomes animated, gesturing and cooing, Helen follows his lead, raising head and eyebrows, and opening her mouth wide.

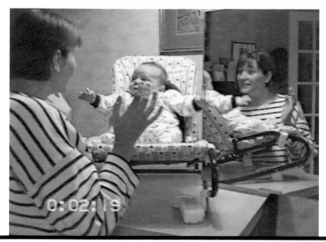

6 ...and then follows his gestures with her hands.

7 Their arms relax together and they both pause.

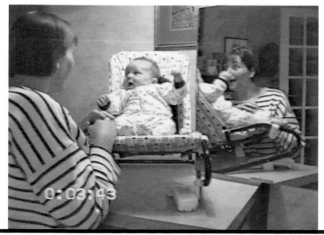

10 The build-up of her own expressions is timed to coincide with the peak of William's communicative efforts...

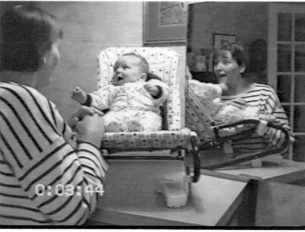

11 ...and they share the enjoyment of being in harmony.

continues over the page

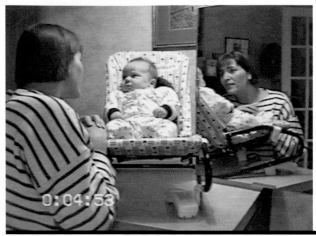

12 William is serious and Helen looks at him enquiringly...

continued from previous page

13 ...signalling her acceptance with a gentle encouraging tone.

16 A few seconds later, and William's expression has brightened; Helen follows his change of mood with a smile.

17 Helen's smile broadens as William's active enjoyment of the conversation intensifies...

20 They have played face-to-face together for several minutes now, and the final phrase is about to begin. William watches, as Helen invites him to play.

21 He responds, smiling and shaping his mouth, and Helen encourages him further.

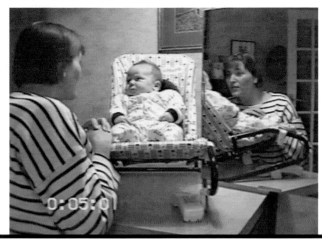

14 As William's frown deepens, Helen picks up on his serious mood...

15 ...and attends carefully as he begins to make active mouthing movements, seeming to tell her what the problem is.

18 ...both turn away slightly and break gaze at the peak of their excitement...

19 ...and then come together to resume their contact, both still smiling broadly.

22 The two share their peak of excitement...

23 ...before relaxing together after a satisfying game.

📽 *Picture story*

BABIES DISLIKE INTRUSIVE SOCIAL CONTACTS

Isabelle, 1 week

Babies are highly sensitive to their social partner's communication. If the response is made abruptly, or before the baby is ready, this can interfere with the baby's engagement, and cause her to break contact.

1 Isabelle is just one week old. Alert and contented, her head well supported, she is ready to have her first social interaction with Liz.

5 ...she frowns and grimaces...

SIGNALS THAT THE BABY IS TIRING

Alexandra B, 2½ weeks

Babies often put a lot of energy into their social interactions, and at some point they may begin to tire. As well as yawns, frowns and grimaces, one sign that the baby may need a break is when she turns away.

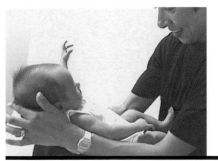

1 Alexandra has been enjoying a long chat with her mother, Shireen, gesturing...

2 ...and making active tonguing and mouthing movements.

2 Isabelle watches Liz's face intently, opens her mouth and moves her tongue. The distance between their faces is just right for Isabelle.

3 Liz starts to move her face nearer while Isabelle is still actively communicating.

4 As Liz moves in, too close for Isabelle, her expression changes, and Isabelle becomes more serious…

6 …and turns away, shutting her eyes.

7 As Liz continues to try to engage with her, Isabelle steadfastly twists away, keeping her eyes shut. The opportunity for play is, for the moment, lost.

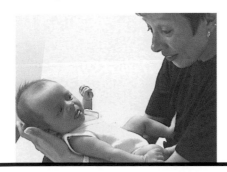  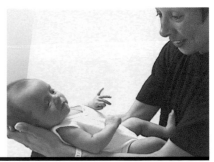

3 As Shireen talks to her, Alexandra still shows her sociability in her tonguing, but she also signals that she wants to reduce her contact, turning her head slightly away and, for the moment, watching Shireen out of the corner of her eye.

4 Now Alexandra cuts her gaze completely. Her mother is respectful of Alexandra's communication, and quietly watches as her daughter takes a break.

5 Now recharged, Alexandra begins to make herself available again for rather less animated social contact.

📽 *Picture story*

THE BABY'S ORDINARY SOCIAL ENCOUNTERS: BREAKING AND MAKING CONTACTS

Alexandra B, 7 weeks

Although a baby is highly sensitive to the way in which her partner responds to her expressions and gestures, playing does not have to be mechanically perfect. Minor incidents, where contact is momentarily broken, are a normal part of the baby's experience. Provided they do not dominate the interaction, these brief irregularities, and their repair, give the baby opportunities to develop her own abilities to manage the influx of stimulation. Episodes of this kind often occur with enthusiastic siblings, who are fascinated by the baby's remarkable capabilities, and extremely keen to connect with them.

Tom, Alexandra's older brother, has collected some musical toys together and he is hoping that Alexandra will like them. For the moment he has placed some bells in her hand. Over the weeks, Alexandra has had a chance to become familiar with her siblings' robust play.

1 Alexandra lies watching her brother, Tom. Her expressions, as well as her active mouthing and kicking, suggest she is ready to play.

4 ...before turning away. Tom is sensitive to this change in his sister's behaviour; he pauses in his active attempts to engage with her...

7 Alexandra seems to be cutting out stimulation as she continues to look away; Tom decides that a different sound might help, and shakes a maraca.

2 Tom eagerly responds to Alexandra's 'invitation'; as he bends down to talk, Alexandra's mouth widens, and her legs move even more energetically.

3 Tom is keen to engage with his baby sister, so he enthusiastically tries out something he has seen Alexandra herself do when being sociable: he puts out his tongue. His response, being so eager, comes before Alexandra is quite ready, and she stills and becomes sombre...

5 ...and withdraws a little. As he does so, Alexandra looks back, and is more receptive...

6 ...but she is not yet quite up to Tom's next approach.

8 Alexandra turns in the direction of the new sound, and the bells fall from her grasp as she attends to what her brother is doing.

9 Tom delights in having attracted his sister's attention and they listen to the sound of the maraca together.

continues over the page

📽 *Picture story*
BREAKING AND MAKING CONTACTS *continued from previous page*

10 Now Tom changes tack; it has occurred to him that he and Alexandra could make music together. Alexandra looks on as Tom prepares the bells.

11 Having them placed around her head is quite a major intrusion, but Alexandra is very robust, and although she startles and frowns a little, she does not become distressed.

12 Alexandra continues to tolerate the bells on her head, and although her arm movements show some agitation, her frown fades…

16 …and helps Alexandra to curl her fingers around the handle of a new set of bells. Alexandra remains unperturbed as she watches what her brother is doing.

17 Appearing almost unaware of the new instrument, Alexandra focuses on her brother's face…

18 …and she starts to become social again, protruding her tongue…

19 Tom enjoys this playful encounter so much …

20 …that he cannot resist leaning over to give his sister a kiss.

21 This is just a little too much and Alexandra turns away; she shuts out the environment very effectively, and Tom's attempt to get a response by tickling her cheek is to no avail.

13 ...and she is able to attend while Tom takes up the maraca again.

14 Alexandra's part in the concert proves problematic as the bells slip from her forehead, but she remains unruffled and calm throughout.

15 Tom decides to try a change of instrument...

22 Eventually, Alexandra is ready to respond again, and she turns animatedly once more to her brother as he tries to draw her in by playing a tonguing game.

23 On this occasion, the kiss is well-timed and Alexandra remains happily engaged.

WELL-ESTABLISHED GAME ROUTINES

'Let's play that one again!'

As face-to-face interactions occur repeatedly over the weeks, events within them that seem to give the baby particular pleasure tend to take on the quality of a routine act that can be enjoyed and shared. So, towards the end of the first three months, parents and others closely involved with the baby may know that certain elements of social play with their baby can be more or less guaranteed to raise a smile when the climax comes. Common examples are body games such as 'round and round the garden', or even very simple routines, like the looming in of the partner's face to touch the baby's tummy. These may start gently, the baby quite seriously watching the partner's face; then the partner gradually helps to build up the sense of anticipation, holding the baby's gaze and monitoring her readiness throughout, using voice, facial expression, and widening of the eyes to mark the imminent arrival of the final climax, when the high point of emotion is shared together. In this way, the face-to-face conversations develop from simply focussing on what the baby may be feeling or thinking, to having a definite structure and topic.

The structure of games also changes towards the end of the first three months as the baby's vision develops. Whereas the baby could previously focus clearly only at a close range, from around three months there is a shift in the development of the visual system, and she begins to be able to focus on things that are at a distance. The baby's attention may then be caught, for example, by some attractive toy that is out of reach. Now, rather than play games that are confined to being face-to-face, the baby may turn away from her parent, and instead show that she is interested in the toy. As the parent follows the baby's cues and fetches the toy, a different kind of game takes place, in which the parent uses the baby's signs of interest and pleasure in the object to hold her attention. The baby may not be able to reach out and grab hold of things effectively for another few weeks, but she can still enjoy swiping at an object and the fun of watching a toy perform antics as her parent manipulates it.

The baby will quickly pick up the sequence of events in new body games like 'round and round the garden', and in set games with toys or other objects. Having rehearsed a game a few times so that it is familiar and predictable, the parent will notice that much of the subsequent enjoyment comes from playing around with elements of uncertainty or surprise, like the timing of the climax, rather than simply repeating the sequence exactly as before. Babies are natural problem-solvers, and enjoy figuring out what the rules are, and then, within the context of the safety of play, how they can be broken!

Other routines in the baby's daily care will also, by this time, have become well-established – such as the way the parent changes the baby's nappy, or gives a feed. As the baby's world becomes more predictable, she will be able to sense what is coming next, and may begin, for example, to show excited anticipation as preparations for a feed are made. This anticipation of what is coming next can also help the baby begin to tolerate waiting, in a way that wasn't possible earlier on. In such small ways, daily, repeated routines accumulate to build up the baby's sense of a predictable, familiar world that embeds her firmly in the particular culture of her own family.

🎥 *Picture story*

THE BEGINNINGS OF WELL-ESTABLISHED GAMES

Catriona, 11 weeks

Catriona is almost three months old. Over the weeks she and her mother, Rachael, have grown accustomed to playing games together, and Catriona has recently started to enjoy a number of set routines. These typically involve the use of Rachael's fingers, or her face looming in to build up to a shared climax: a tickle under the arm, for example, a touch on the nose, or a tickle under the chin.

With a baby of this age, social engagements are not concerned simply with the two partners sharing their feelings and experience: they take on a separate topic; they are 'about something'.

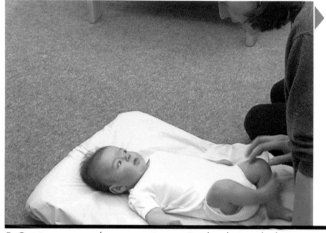

1 Catriona pays close attention as Rachael signals that a game is about to start.

4 The two share the final moments of anticipation…

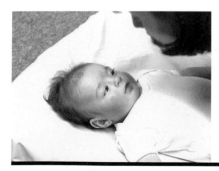

1 Catriona smiles as another familiar routine begins – the 'loom and tickle' game.

2 Her eyes start to widen as she watches her mother get into position for the approach.

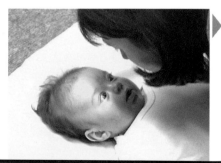

3 Catriona's excitement intensifies as her mother closes in.

2 Catriona knows this routine well, and as Rachael's fingers begin to move up her leg, she starts to become excited, her mouth opening and her eyes widening.

3 Catriona's pleasure and excitement grow as the fingers move on, her eyes locked on to her mother's face.

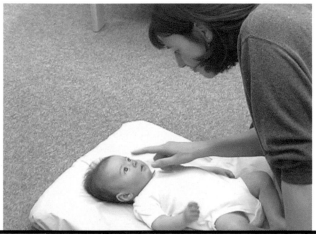

5 …then Catriona stills as she registers the climax…

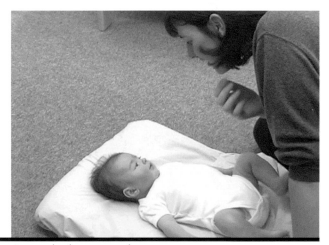

6 …and relaxes now the moment is over.

4 They share the fun as contact is almost made.

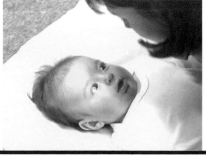

5 Catriona's excitement builds up again in preparation for the climax they both know will come…

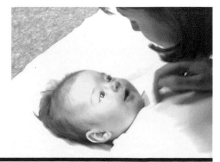

6 …the tickle under the chin!

🎥 *Picture story*   GAMES WITH A TOPIC: 'COO' AND 'BOO'

Ethan, 11 weeks

By around three months, babies can play face-to-face games that are often robust, vigorous and exciting affairs. They often take on a 'topic' for play – this can include jokes, as the two partners 'muck about' and watch each other's reactions. Two games are especial hits these days with Ethan and Julie – 'coo' and 'boo'. In 'coo', Ethan takes the initiative, and enjoys using the full force of his voice to create an impact on his mother. In 'boo', it is Julie who performs, while Ethan watches with anticipation and then enjoys sharing the climax with her.

1 Julie pays close attention as Ethan starts to coo.

4 Now it is Julie's turn – Ethan watches his mother get ready – Ah...

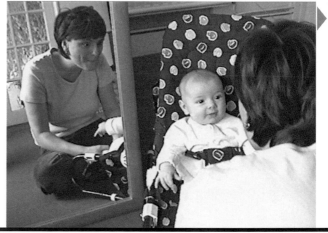

5 ...Bb...

8 Ethan coos to Julie again...

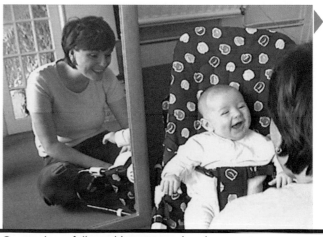

9 ...and it is followed by raucous laughter.

(To take these pictures with just one camera, we placed a mirror next to Ethan.)

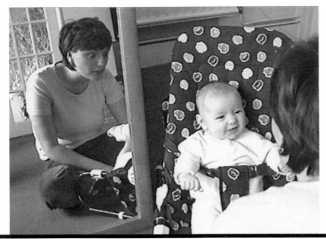

2 His call is forceful and is directed right at Julie; she shows how impressed she is.

3 Ethan seems to feel the punch line is hilarious!

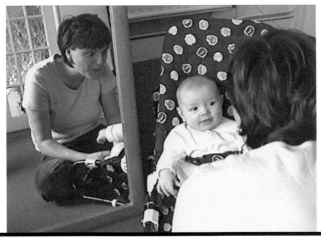

6 ...Boo!...

7 ...and Ethan is duly appreciative, joining in with Julie's laughter.

10 Now Julie boos at Ethan – he's already finding it fun...

11 ...but is even more delighted as Julie laughs too.

☷ *Picture story*

GAMES WITH A TOPIC: 'WALKING FINGERS TICKLE'

Ethan, 11 weeks

(To take these pictures with just one camera, we placed a mirror next to Ethan.)

As well as simple single-action routines like 'coo' and 'boo', games at around three months can be more sophisticated and involve several distinct stages. Typically, there is some introductory stage-setting, then a build-up of excitement to the final climax. Common examples are finger and tickle games like, 'round and round the garden', or 'this little piggy'. As the baby becomes familiar with these games, she will actively participate, anticipating each step, and sharing the fun of the climax. Timing becomes everything, and games work best when each step is finely tuned to the baby's level of attention and engagement. Here Julie simply walks her fingers up Ethan's tummy, and then tickles him under his chin.

3 Ethan monitors Julie's expression closely, as her fingers begin their familiar ascent up his tummy.

6 ...and wriggles with pleasure as the final moment comes.

1 Julie signals the start of a familiar finger game, checking to see that Ethan has registered it. His bright look to Julie's face shows that he is fully attentive.

2 As Julie lowers her eyes, and moves her hand into position, Ethan's eyes widen, and his arms move excitedly, anticipating one of his favourite games.

4 Still watching Julie, Ethan tenses in anticipation as the climax approaches.

5 As the tickling is about to start, he breaks into a smile...

7 When the tickling stops, Ethan's role shifts from being at the receiving end of the game to actively expressing his appreciation...

8 ...and he coos to his mother, as though applauding the fun they have had.

Picture story

EACH KIND OF CONTACT HAS ITS OWN TIME AND PLACE

Cody, 7 weeks

Knowing just what will work to engage the baby is not always easy, particularly for those whose contacts with her are sporadic or, as can often be the case with a young child, when enthusiasm, coupled with immaturity, takes over.

Cody is only seven weeks old, and he has not yet begun to appreciate structured games. His sister Ellie, is, however, determined to try out 'round and round the garden'. Cody would rather play 'face-to-face' and is ignoring his big sister's efforts. He makes a bid for his mother's attention. Cody's mother, Beki, sensitively sets up the conditions for a more satisfying encounter between her son and daughter, and Ellie is thrilled to find how responsive her baby brother can be.

1 Cody looks glum as his sister, Ellie, takes his hand and starts to play 'round and round the garden'.

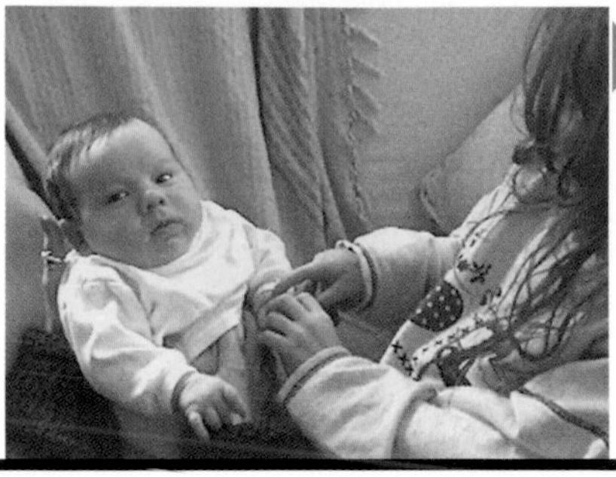

2 Ellie's efforts are in vain – Cody steadfastly ignores her, turning instead to his mother...

6 The children's mother, Beki, knows how much Ellie wants to play with her baby brother, and she shifts Cody so that the children are in a better position to engage with one another.

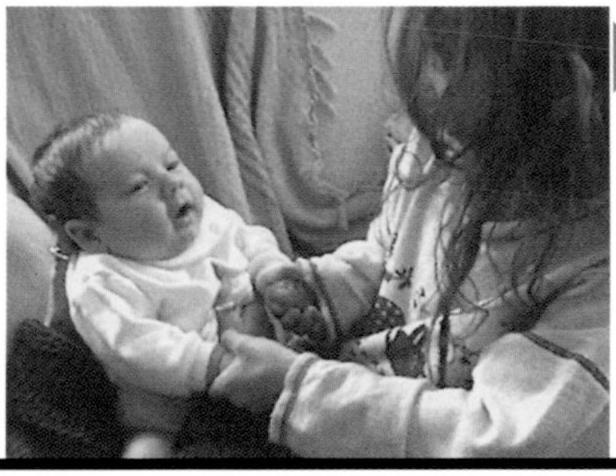

7 Cody responds to this new opportunity; he gazes at Ellie and shapes his mouth and coos.

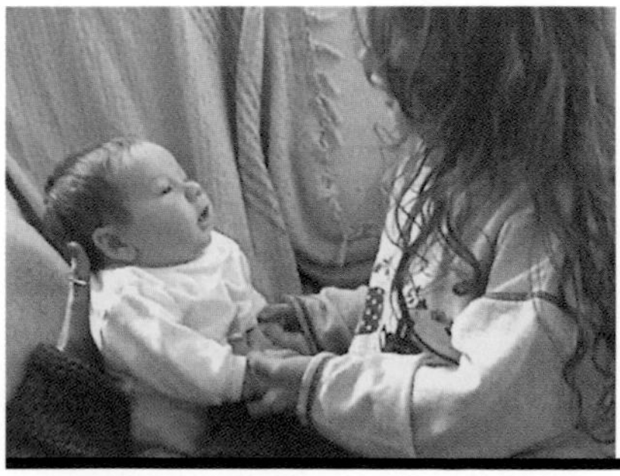

9 ...and he looks alert and fully engaged.

10 Now it is Ellie's turn to talk, and Cody watches for some seconds...

3 ...even as the game progresses...

4 ...to its climax.

5 Cody would much rather play with someone face-to-face, and he tries to engage with his mother, actively mouthing and making hand gestures.

8 Cody's active efforts to communicate continue; his tongue is very mobile...

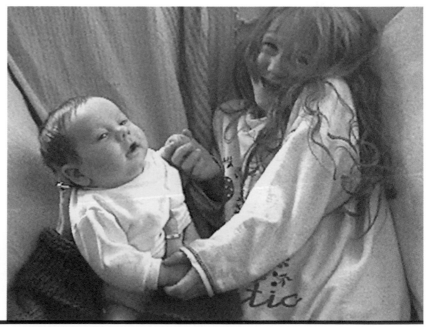

11 ...before taking back the initiative and resuming his 'pre-speech' mouthing.

12 The game is over, and both Cody and Ellie turn to their mother, Ellie feeling proud of her success with her brother.

🎥 *Picture story*
'I'LL GOBBLE YOU UP!'
Cody, 4 months

Cody is some weeks older now, and he is much more able to take part in body games. He and his mother, Beki, have developed a number of routines around the theme of 'I'll gobble you up'.

1 Beki checks to see that Cody is ready for play.

4 ...for the climax...

5 ...and then relaxes in laughter with his mother.

8 Cody tilts his head back in anticipation....and...

9 ...waits with bated breath...

2 As she opens her mouth and lowers her head in the direction of Cody's foot, he laughs in recognition.

3 Cody's feeling of suspense builds up, as he waits...

6 Cody braces himself for another approach.

7 He takes part in the build-up, opening his mouth wide in concert with Beki.

10 ...for the 'gobble, gobble'...

11 ...and wriggles with pleasure at the end.

📽 *Picture story*

THE SHIFT TOWARDS PLAY WITH OBJECTS

Ethan, 11 weeks

(To take these pictures with just one camera, we placed a mirror next to Ethan.)

As Ethan approaches three months, his vision improves, and he is becoming able to see things in focus that are at a distance. This development coincides with a further change in the structure of play. The baby may now tire of simple, face-to-face communication, and find some nearby object more appealing. This change in the focus of the attention can prompt the parent to bring new objects into the arena of their play. This is one of the ways in which play changes from being purely concerned with the sharing of the feelings and experience of the two participants, to having a separate topic.

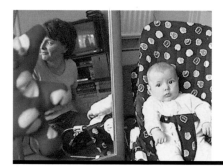

2 Julie follows the direction of Ethan's gaze to see what has attracted him...

3 ...and she reaches out to the toy.

4 Ethan, meanwhile, remains transfixed.

8 Julie places it in Ethan's grasp...

9 ...and he manages to hold on to it.

10 Now Julie squeezes the starfish, causing it to squeak. Ethan looks up at his mother as he hears the unexpected noise.

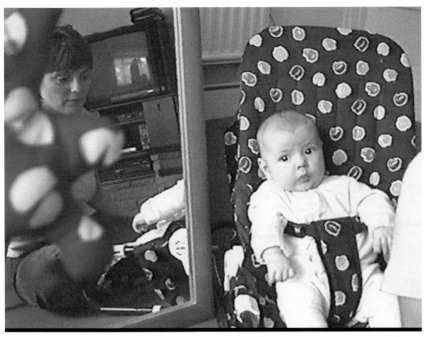

1 Ethan's attention to his mother is beginning to flag, and is suddenly caught by a red and white toy starfish.

5 Julie brings the starfish up to Ethan.

6 He looks at it intently, concentrating hard.

7 Ethan is enraptured, and stretches out his hands to the starfish.

11 He enjoys his mother's mock surprise...

12 ...and, while holding the starfish, he continues to watch his mother as she makes it squeak again.

13 Now Ethan and Julie are sharing not just their enjoyment of each other, but the fun of sharing their experience of the wider world.

CHAPTER TWO

THE BABY'S PHYSICAL WORLD

RELATING TO THE PHYSICAL WORLD
Babies' early abilities

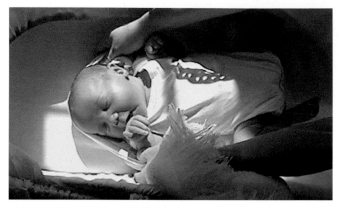

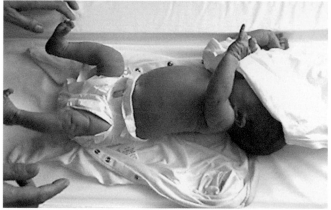

An understanding of the way in which babies interact with the physical world can be helpful to parents in organising their baby's environment. In fact, even in the first few weeks, babies know quite a lot about the physical world. The fact that the newborn will turn towards someone's voice shows that she can locate herself in physical space in relation to the sounds around her. The baby also very soon realises that things she can see, even if it is for the first time, have physical substance. For example, if an object is moved towards the baby, looming up as though it might make contact with the baby's face, the baby will turn away, or move her arms up defensively in front of her face. Similarly, the baby can also sense whether something she can see matches what she can feel or touch. A baby who has had a dummy with a particular texture placed in her mouth, without having caught sight of it, and who is then shown two objects, one with the same texture as the dummy, and one that is different, will choose to look more at the matching surface. It is as though the baby's world is one in which the different senses are already connected to one another, so that the baby does not have to learn these associations from experience. This is what Aristotle called 'common sense'!

As well as sensing these properties of the physical world, small babies can do a number of things for themselves. They can turn their head towards or away from a stimulus, such as a bright light; some of them may even be able to swipe away a light cover that has fallen across their eyes. And they can track a slowly moving object with head and eye movements. Some are even robust enough to do a rudimentary crawl! If the baby is alert and contented, and her head is well supported, she will, even when just a few days old, reach out to an object in front of her. She will not be able to deliberately reach out and grasp it for some months, but nevertheless she will position and shape her hands appropriately.

Babies also come to the world wanting to figure out how it works, and in particular to learn how they can make things happen. They are born problem-solvers. Even within the first few weeks, the baby can learn how to turn her head from side to side, or kick her legs in a series of movements so that some interesting event is triggered, like a light flashing, or a mobile set in motion. As she discovers that she can control what is happening, she is likely to become more excited, and from about two months, she will even start to coo and smile during these games. Eventually, having thoroughly mastered what the connection is between her activity and the event, the baby is likely to lose interest, and she will start engaging in the game again only if some change is made.

🎥 *Picture story*

NATASHA LISTENS AND TURNS IN THE DIRECTION OF THE SOUND

Natasha, 1 week

Babies can locate themselves in physical space in relation to the sounds around them. A simple rattle can be made with a cocktail stick box containing some maize kernels, that is sealed shut with adhesive tape. A quick vigorous shake will make a high-frequency noise that will attract the baby's attention.

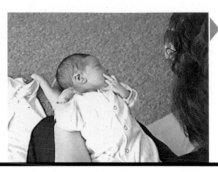

1 Natasha concentrates on Liz's face. Out to the side, where Natasha cannot see it, Liz shakes the home-made rattle with its high-frequency noise.

2 Natasha immediately turns to locate the source of the interesting sound.

NATASHA WATCHES, LISTENS AND TRACKS THE RATTLE

Natasha, 1 week

Now Liz keeps the rattle in Natasha's view, and moves it slowly to and fro, shaking it as she does so, and allowing Natasha to hear as well as see the object. Natasha's attention is held for some minutes by the home-made toy; she tracks it with head and eyes, and although she is not actually able to reach out and take hold of the rattle, her hands are active, and she shapes her fingers in pincer, grasping movements.

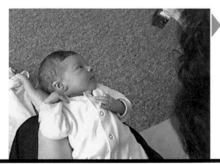

1 Liz establishes that Natasha is watching the toy, at first holding it in Natasha's central field of vision.

2

6 As the toy slowly sweeps a fresh arc, Natasha again raises her left hand…

7 …and she makes another pincer, grasping movement with her fingers…

3 The sound ceases, and Natasha turns back to look at Liz.

4 Now Liz shakes the unseen rattle on the other side...

5 ...and Natasha turns accordingly in the other direction to locate the sound again.

3

4 Natasha watches as the rattle is moved in a wide arc; she coordinates her head and eye movements to keep it in view...

5 ...at the same time, she raises her arms, opening her hands and then curling her fingers, her left hand making a pincer, grasping movement.

8

9 ...before her arm falls, and the rattle passes beyond her reach.

⏺ *Picture story*

SWIPING A VEST AWAY FROM THE FACE

Natasha, 1 week

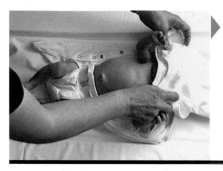

1 Liz gently places a vest so that it covers Natasha's face.

SAFETY WARNING

It is, of course, essential to the baby that nothing interferes with her breathing. It is also important to her that her eyes are not covered. Carefully monitoring Natasha during a paediatric examination, Liz demonstrates how well this baby is able to look after herself, as Natasha succeeds in removing a vest which Liz places lightly over her eyes. Babies differ, however, in how well they cope with such situations, and parents should always ensure that their baby's breathing is not obstructed when they are dressing or undressing a baby, for example.

This demonstration of Natasha's powerful urge to breathe freely, and see, and her ability to swipe away the vest, is based on Dr Berry Brazelton's Neonatal Behavioural Assessment Scale, and should be performed only by trained practitioners.

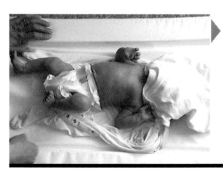

5 She starts to take hold of the vest with her left hand…

CODY AND HIS HAT

Cody, 7 weeks

Just how important it is to the baby that her vision is not obscured is shown in this naturally occuring situation when Cody's hat slips over his eyes. He immediately starts to twist and turn, arching his back and taking swipes at the offending object. His facial expressions show how unpleasant he finds the experience. With much wriggling and effort, Cody succeeds in nudging his hat up so that he is free to look around.

1 Cody's hat has slipped over his eyes.

2 He grimaces, clearly finding this unpleasant, and he twists to one side…

3 …and then the other, his hands shooting up.

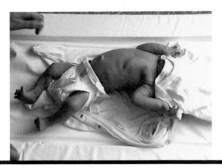

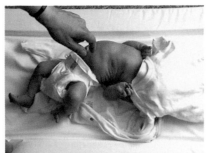

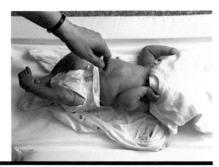

2 Natasha's arms shoot up to the vest and she squirms and twists.

3 Natasha arches her back right up.

4 Her back-arching hasn't shaken off the vest, so Natasha now begins to use her hands.

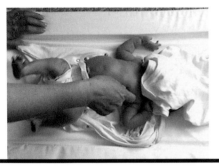

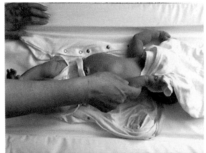

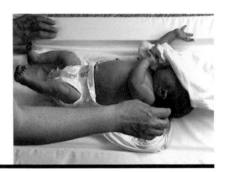

6 ...and now she has gripped it firmly...

7 ...and begins to tug the vest down.

8 Natasha succeeds in swiping the vest clear of her face.

4 Now he rubs his head against his seat, and succeeds in pushing the edge of his hat up.

5 Cody has managed to remove his hat from his left eye; now he wriggles some more and takes a swipe with his right hand.

18 At last he can see.

HOW DOES ALL THIS AFFECT PARENTS?

Adjusting the environment to meet the baby's needs

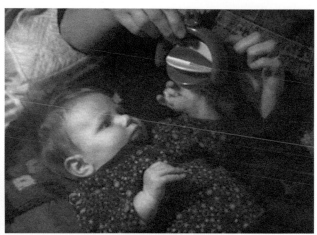

Despite babies' remarkable capacities to respond to their physical environment when they are small, they have to rely on those who care for them to take note of their responses, and to help them in their dealings with the world. For example, if a baby shows some interest in a particular object, this interest can best be satisfied if a person who understands the baby holds the object at the right distance for the baby to be able to focus on it. Similarly, if a baby finds the light from a window too bright and disturbing, the person who understands the baby's expressions and movements could turn the baby's chair around, or draw the curtains. In order for babies to have the sort of environment they want and need, it is necessary for someone to be there to read their signals of interest, attention, or distress, and to respond appropriately. Parents can be helped to read these signals by knowing more about how young infants deal with the different kinds of stimulation they receive from the world.

In the first weeks of life, babies are especially attracted to particular kinds of visual stimulation. For example, apart from people's faces, they will look intently at patterns that have strong, clear contrasts, such as a stripy black and white design, or a checkerboard. The border of a window frame or a picture may also catch their eye and hold their attention.

The best distance for the baby to be able to focus in the first few weeks is 22cm (9in). This is just the kind of distance the baby's face will be from that of the person who is feeding her, and the distance at which people intuitively tend to place themselves when talking to a baby. It is also the best distance at which to hold an object that will capture and hold the baby's attention, or at which to place a mobile or picture so that the baby can look at it on her own.

Of course the most effective opportunity for the baby to be able to sense connections between her own activity and events in the world is, as we have seen, during interactions with a partner who is responsive and sensitive to the baby's cues. The fact that people intuitively respond by mirroring back what the baby does in the first few weeks, often displaying enriched versions of the baby's original expression (for example, through vocalising as well as mimicking the facial movement) not only taps into the baby's inborn ability to connect the different sensory systems, but it also enables her to discover how she can influence the world.

Similarly, as the partner monitors the baby's level of interest as it waxes and wanes during face-to-face play, they are perfectly placed to adjust their behaviour, providing variation as well as theme, so that the baby's attention is recaptured as she tries to master the new rules of the game. However, parents cannot always be available to play with their baby, but setting up patterned mobiles, or toys or objects that are suspended within swiping distance, can help to involve the baby and add to her interest in her environment, long before she can reach out and grasp things, or move around independently.

🎥 *Picture story*
SENSITIVITY TO THE ENVIRONMENT

1. SUDDEN NOISE
Events that cause hardly a blink or a wince in an adult can provoke a strong response in a young baby. In the first example, the sound of a door banging in the wind caused Alexandra to startle.

2. BRIGHT LIGHT
In the second example, the room lighting in the research unit caused Emily distress. Noticing the baby's signs of distress, and whether it occurs in response to different stimulation, can help parents think about how to manage the baby's environment.

3. BRIGHT LIGHT
In the third example, the baby's distress when something is wrong is powerfully conveyed in her facial expression and body movements. These provide important signals to guide the parents in providing the care their baby needs.

2 *Emily D, 2 weeks*

1 Emily winces, as she lies on her back – the ceiling light nearby is causing her trouble...

2 ...and her distress rapidly escalates.

3 As one of the room lights is turned off, her crying abates, although she keeps her eyes tightly shut.

3 *Isabelle, 1 week*

1 Isabelle is enjoying being carried around by her father, Nigel.

2 Inadvertently, Nigel moves so that the light shines directly into Isabelle's eyes. She winces, and shuts her eyes tight...

3 ...and squirms, causing Nigel to startle.

1 *Alexandra B, 2 weeks*

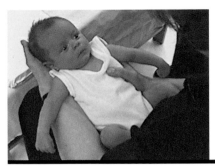

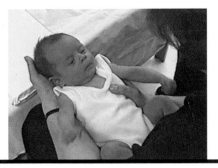

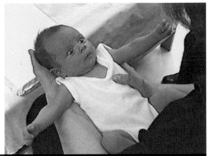

1 Alexandra lies on Liz's lap, quite serious but relaxed.

2 As the door bangs, Alexandra blinks, and within a fraction of a second...

3 ...her arms are thrown out in a startle response, and her eyes widen in shock. What may seem a relatively trivial event was, for Alexandra, a significant disruption.

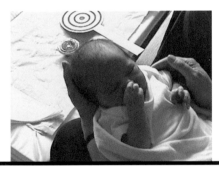

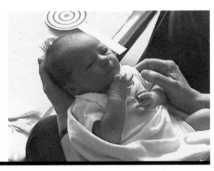

4 Now the second room light is turned off: Emily, with her eyes still closed, calms further, aided by the comfort of her thumb.

5 Now that the lights are extinguished, and she has calmed herself, she can begin to relate to the world again. Her eyes are open, and she no longer needs to suck.

6 She is ready to engage with Liz.

4 Nigel is drawn to attend to Isabelle as she grimaces and tries to turn away from the light...

5 ...and he becomes concerned at his daughter's evident distress.

6 Nigel takes immediate action: he moves away from the light, and Isabelle calms down and opens her eyes again.

📽 *Picture story*
LOLLIPOP-WATCHING 1

Helping the baby to enjoy physical objects is not always straightforward, even if the object is one like the lollipop (shown here) that is perfectly designed to match babies' visual capacities. Whether or not the baby will readily engage with it depends on a range of factors. These include her state of alertness, and how overloaded she may feel by other stimulation; her age and maturity will also be relevant. Such individual differences between babies will affect the way the parent can present objects to the baby and help her enjoy the experience.

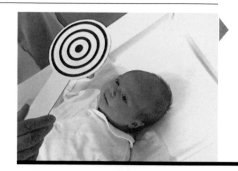

Emily D, 1 week

Emily is quiet and alert as she becomes captivated by the lollipop, with its clear black and white design. As it is moved slowly from side to side, Emily's head and eye movements are perfectly coordinated, allowing her to track the lollipop and keep it in view. There are moments when Emily becomes quite excited; she breathes more quickly, and her movements become vigorous, occasionally stretching out towards the lollipop. Emily remains fascinated by the lollipop for some minutes, before she finally loses interest and turns away, signalling that she has had enough.

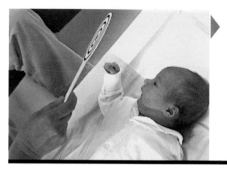

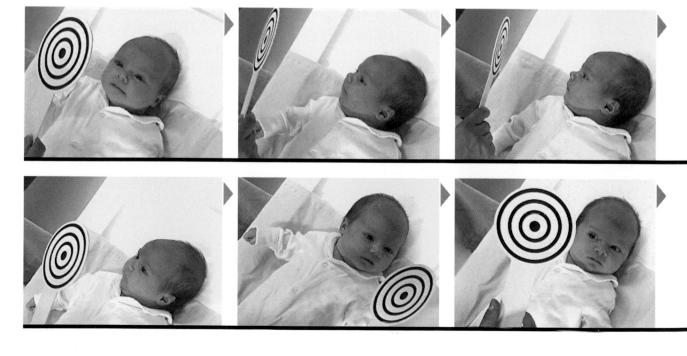

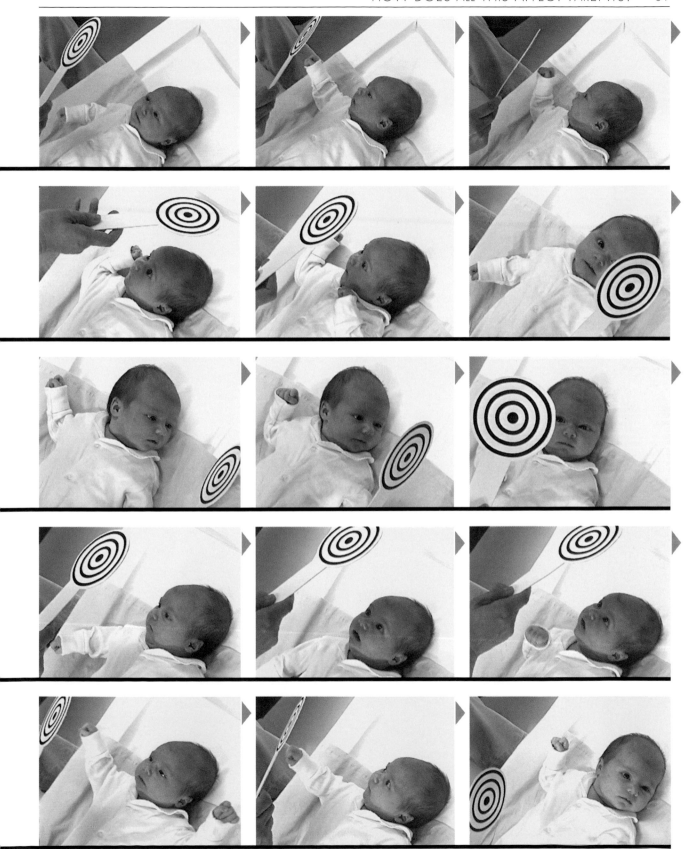

continues over the page

LOLLIPOP-WATCHING 2

Natasha, 1 week

Natasha was born at 36 weeks' gestation. Possibly because she was born a little prematurely, she can find it quite difficult to sustain her attention, and to coordinate her head and eyes to keep the lollipop in view as it is slowly moved to and fro in front of her.

1 Natasha gazes intently at a new face as Liz holds her.

2 Liz introduces the lollipop and slowly moves it up and down within Natasha's range of vision.

3 Natasha's subsequent behaviour suggests she finds the stimulation difficult to manage…she squirms and grimaces…

JUST ONE MINUTE LATER…

Having cut herself off for a few seconds, Natasha is now much more able to enjoy the lollipop, and it immediately captures her attention as Liz introduces it again. Liz helps Natasha by adjusting the lollipop to keep it in Natasha's line of vision. Eventually, however, Natasha loses interest in the object; instead, her attention is caught by Liz's face, and she gazes at her steadily, now ready for social interaction.

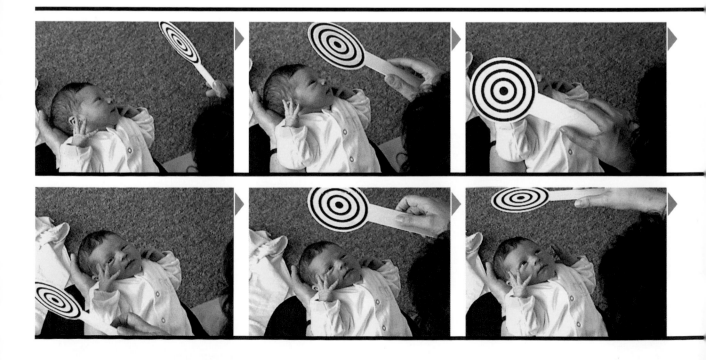

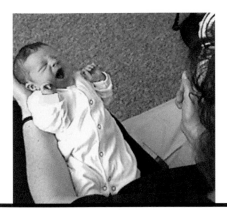

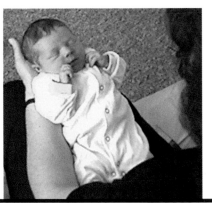

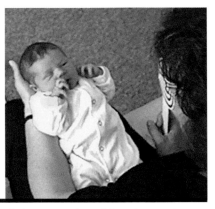

4 ...and she yawns, then closes her eyes and draws her hands up to her face, making herself unavailable.

5 Liz offers no stimulation, allowing Natasha to take a break.

6 A moment later Natasha monitors the situation, opening one eye, and looking at Liz. She is good at controlling the level of incoming stimulation so that it is manageable.

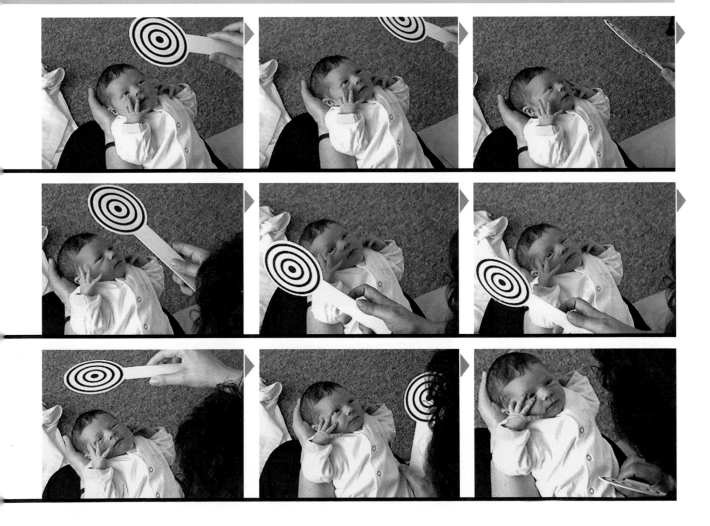

CHAPTER THREE

CRYING AND CONSOLING

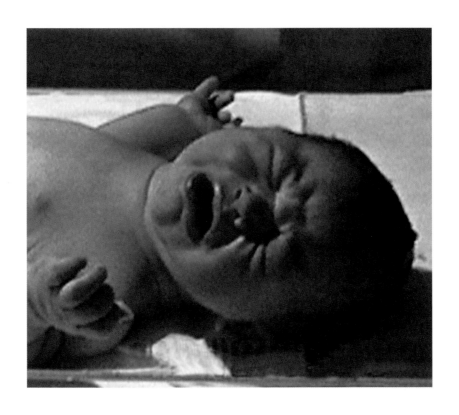

DEVELOPMENTAL CHANGES IN CRYING
General patterns and variability

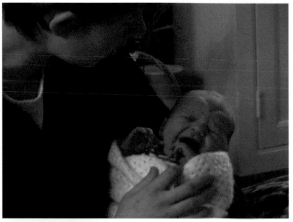

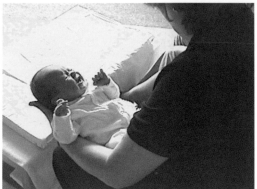

GENERAL DEVELOPMENTAL PATTERN

Crying is the baby's most obvious means of attracting parents' attention and securing their care, and it is therefore an important part of the baby's communication. However, in the beginning it is not always easy for parents to tell from the sound of the cry itself just what the reason is for the crying. The quality of the cry signals the baby's general degree of distress, or urgency, but parents use several cues, such as facial expressions and body movements, as well as the context, to try to work out the particular reason. For example, at first, crying may be easily misinterpreted as a signal that the baby is hungry. However, with growing familiarity with the baby's rooting and sucking behaviour in different situations, parents will be able to distinguish a hunger cry from one for other reasons (see p.146 for Rooting and Sucking).

Crying is a common source of stress and difficulty for parents, and at times such stress can feel overwhelming. When the baby's crying is felt to be excessive, it is a frequent reason for parents taking their babies to the doctor in the early months. In general, the amount of time that babies spend crying increases over the first few weeks, and then declines. The most common peak in the total amount of time spent crying is between three and six weeks when babies will cry and fret, on average, for a little more than two hours a day. Much of this crying occurs in the late afternoon or evening.

Studies of crying in different countries show similar patterns in terms of the time of day and the age at which the peak rate occurs, in spite of very different child-rearing practices. From around three months to the end of the first year, the daily amount of crying generally declines to about one hour a day, mainly because of a reduction in the amount of evening crying – some research has shown that it declines steadily at the rate of just over one minute a day, for each week that passes!

VARIATIONS IN THE GENERAL PATTERN

In spite of the general patterns described above in the timing and amount of crying, it is important to be aware that there are wide variations in how much babies cry. For one thing, there are striking day-to-day fluctuations in the amount of crying, especially in the newborn period.

The age at which crying peaks also varies. Most notable from the parents' point of view is the fact that the length of time spent crying per day varies between babies. A sizeable proportion of babies (around 20%) fuss and cry for more than three hours per day on at least three days per week. These babies are particularly prone to cry in the evenings, but even their daytime crying times are longer than the average, and for many the crying is particularly intense. Such behaviour is fairly stable early on, so that babies who cry persistently in the first two weeks are more likely than others still to be crying for substantial amounts of time at three months. After the early months, however, this stable pattern changes, and the fact that a baby cries more than usual in the first few weeks does not mean that she will still be a child who cries a lot when she is one year old.

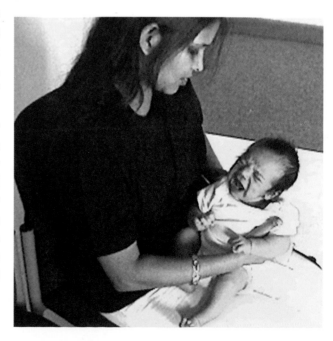

WHY SOME BABIES CRY MORE THAN OTHERS
Theories and evidence

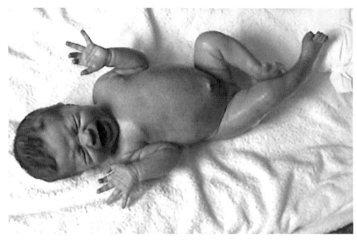

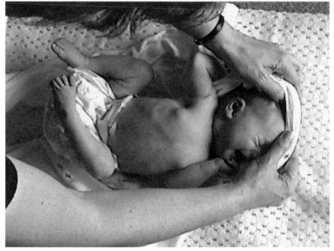

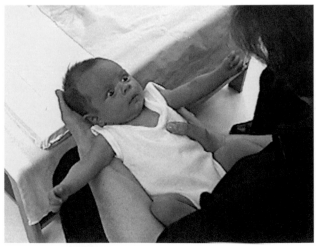

Having a baby who cries easily and persistently can place a tremendous strain on parents and other family members. This is especially so if parents believe that, somehow, they are responsible for the baby's difficult behaviour, or if they have little support, or imagine that other people are judging them harshly.

The reasons why some babies are prone to cry more than others in the first place are still not well understood, and it may simply reflect one end of a spectrum of normal behaviour, rather than the fact that there is anything wrong. A number of common assumptions, including the idea that babies cry more than usual because the parents are inexperienced or are doing something wrong, have been found to be groundless. In fact, first-time parents are no more likely than experienced parents to have a baby who cries more than average in the first three months. Similarly, there is no good evidence that having a baby who cries easily and is difficult to soothe is a consequence of poor parental handling. (Whether or not a baby continues to cry a great deal, or else settles down over the first year, is a different issue. This *can* be affected by how the crying is managed – and this topic is covered further on). Another common misconception is that there are major differences between boys and girls in the amount of early crying whereas, in fact, any such influence seems to be trivial, research having shown that any sex difference is likely to account for only about five minutes of crying per day!

'Colic', or gastrointestinal disturbance, is believed by many parents to be the reason why some babies cry more than others in the first three months, and for a small minority this does seem to be the case. In a minority of cases, 'colic' may be linked to an intolerance of cow's milk protein in either breast or bottle milk, particularly where the parents themselves experience such reactions. Nevertheless, research generally shows that 'colic' is likely to be the reason for excessive crying in only about 10-15% of babies who are seen by doctors for crying problems. Apart from the case of babies who do suffer from colic that is related to a specific dietary intolerance, there is no evidence that feeding method – breast or bottle – is related to the amount that babies cry.

One possible reason for some babies' persistent crying in the first three months is that they have greater difficulty than other babies in coping with shifts and changes, including the shift towards a day-night sleep cycle. These babies may also be particularly sensitive to moment to moment changes in their environment, and find them hard to manage. Everyday experiences, like having a nappy changed, can be stressful at the point where the baby is undressed; or the baby may startle at a sudden noise and she may become quickly disorganised in her behaviour, and distressed. Similarly, the baby who is particularly sensitive in the first few weeks may find it hard to fend off too much stimulation by dampening down her responses, as other babies can. Once they have become unsettled, these babies find it very difficult to become calm again, and they typically need much more help from a parent than other babies. Premature babies are more likely to show these kinds of response than those who are full term, but a number of studies suggest that almost one in five of healthy, well-developed babies, without any neurological abnormality, are highly sensitive in the early weeks.

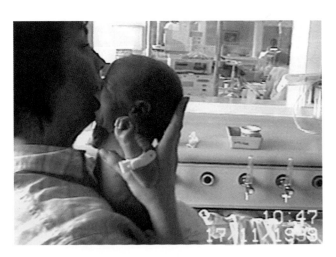

📽 *Picture story*
MANAGING A NEW ENVIRONMENT

Zak, 1 week

Zak is a first-born baby whose home environment is quiet and calm. This is only his second outing, and he finds it hard to cope with the new situation of being in the research unit. Although neither tired nor hungry, Zak spends his first hour in the strange environment in an unsettled, fretful state, and it is hard for his mother, Bina, to help him. Zak resists all attempts to engage with the people around him, and is content only when stimulation is cut right down, and he is given support to suck on his fist.

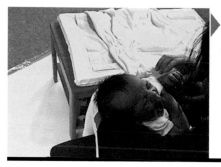

1 Zak is finding it hard to settle in his mother's arms.

5 He manages to find his thumb...

9 As Bina lifts him to look at him face on, he becomes distressed again, his colour changing, as well as his facial expression.

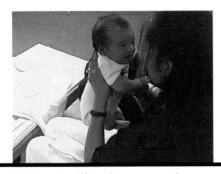

2 Bina tries lifting him up onto her shoulder.

3 Zak calms a little…

4 …and then tries to find something to suck.

6 …and sucks on it in earnest to comfort himself.

7 Bina wants to check to make sure that Zak is happy, and moves him from her shoulder…

8 …and then onto her lap where she can see him. Zak manages to keep a fist to suck, but he quickly frowns.

10 Up on Bina's shoulder, Zak settles once more, and finds his fist…

11 …but as soon as he is moved again to face the world…

12 …he loses his thumb and the support and comfort of his mother's shoulder, and once again becomes upset.

COPING WITH CRYING

Using the baby's cues to prevent distress

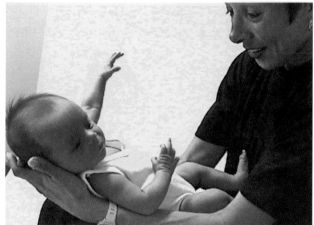

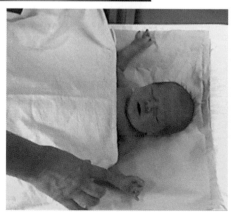

Two key points to bear in mind if parents have a baby who cries a great deal in the first few weeks are, first, that the baby is not a 'bad' baby who will inevitably go on being difficult to manage; and second, that the parents are not to blame for the problem. Parents whose baby cries more than usual do, in fact, deserve extra care and support – from family, friends and professionals, just as their baby does.

LOOKING FOR EARLY SIGNS OF DISTRESS

An essential principle that can help parents cope with their baby's crying is to watch their own baby's unique responses, and to be guided by them. This applies, first and foremost, to noticing subtle changes in expression and behaviour that signal that the baby may be starting to become distressed. These include cues such as squirming and arching the back, yawning or turning away, frowning and grimacing or possetting (see p.108). Noticing these early signals, and taking steps to change or modify whatever is happening, may help to prevent mild distress from escalating.

AVOIDING DIFFICULT SITUATIONS

It is also helpful to be able to anticipate which situations the baby finds difficult to manage. For example, if removing a nappy or other clothing is very distressing (as it often is for sensitive babies in the early weeks), and the baby is unable to calm herself, then having a cover on hand to place over the baby as the nappy is removed may help to make her feel less vulnerable. Similarly, containing the baby's arms may prevent them shooting out and causing the baby to become even more agitated. Some babies hate being naked, and bath times can be intensely stressful for all concerned. Finding other ways to wash the baby until she is ready – 'topping and tailing', for instance – can remove a major source of difficulty. Alternatively, the parents may decide to take the baby with them into the bath, so providing her with the security of being held close throughout.

Similarly, if parents notice that the baby startles and then becomes distressed at sudden noises, like a telephone ringing, it may be helpful to think whether simple practical steps can be taken to prevent such difficulties arising, like changing the arrangement of the furniture, so that the baby is out of earshot of the phone.

Babies often make large 'startle' movements when they are in light sleep and, particularly in the case of sensitive babies, these may be strong enough to cause the baby to wake and then cry. Swaddling these babies when they go to sleep may help to prevent these disruptions to the baby's state (see p.148 for more notes on swaddling).

🎥 *Picture story*

BECOMING FAMILIAR WITH EARLY SIGNS OF DISTRESS

Emilie, 10 days

A baby who is under a month old, if alert and content, will take part in rudimentary 'conversational' engagements. Although her behaviour does not have the same richness and complexity of expression as that of a two-month-old, the basic structure of active participation, alternating between watching and listening, is in place. In the first few weeks, however, the baby may not be able to sustain long periods of engagement, and it can be helpful to the parent to recognise early signs of tiring.

Emilie is just ten days old. She and her father, Pierre, enjoy a 'conversation' in which the balance of initiative shifts between them. At first, Emilie is the more active partner, with Pierre attending carefully to her communication; then Pierre joins in, and it becomes Emilie's turn to watch and listen. After a while Emilie becomes tired, and she begins to switch off. These early signals of fatigue are quite subtle. At this point Pierre is not sure what they mean and he attempts to prolong the engagement. Emilie, however, has had enough, and needs to make this clearer to Pierre, so she starts to cry. At the sound of Emilie's distress, her mother, Stephanie, arrives. Using voice and touch, she manages to settle Emilie off to sleep.

Pierre is able to use this episode to reflect on how Emilie shows early signs of stress. This enables him to watch out for these signs and match his responses to Emilie's in a way that offers them both a more enhanced experience.

3 Emilie continues with her 'pre-speech' communication, and Pierre watches attentively.

6 Now Pierre begins to respond, his smile widening...

COPING WITH CRYING 103

1 Emilie looks at her father intently as he watches a visitor leave.

2 As soon as Pierre turns to her, Emilie starts to engage with him, her mouth actively shaped and her brows raised.

4

5

7 ...and he begins to shape his own mouth, picking up on Emilie's expression...

8 ...for a while they perform together.

continues over the page

🎥 *Picture story*

BECOMING FAMILIAR WITH EARLY SIGNS OF DISTRESS

continued from previous page

9

12

15 She cuts her gaze from Pierre's face...

10 As Pierre repeats his mirroring of Emilie's communication, her mouth relaxes. Only her hand is active as she gestures towards her father, and it is her turn to watch and listen.

11

13

14 Emilie has been engrossed in this conversation for some minutes, and a slight frown suggests she may be beginning to tire.

16 ...squirms, frowns further, and rubs her face. Her father notices, and pauses to see what Emilie will do.

17 Emilie recovers briefly so Pierre continues to engage actively with her...

continues over the page

▶ *Picture story*

BECOMING FAMILIAR WITH EARLY SIGNS OF DISTRESS

continued from previous page

18 …but she really is starting to flag, gives a big yawn, and cuts her gaze once more…

21 …and as she makes a fresh bid to engage, Pierre is once more encouraged to play.

22 Emilie, though, has really had enough. Exhausted, she begins to cry in earnest…

23 …and her mother, Stephanie, comes to see what is happening.

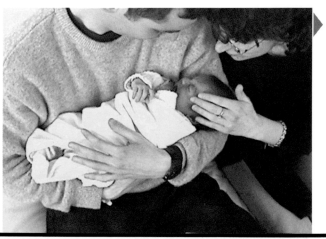

24 While Emilie stays contained in the comfort of her father's arms, Stephanie soothes her daughter, stroking her, and talking gently to her. Emilie responds, and begins to calm.

19 ...and then cries briefly.

20 Yet again Emilie appears to rally...

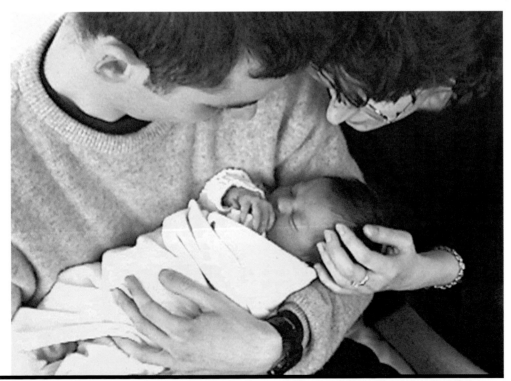

25 After such an active play session, Emilie slips quickly into a deep sleep, enjoying the comfort of her thumb as Pierre continues to cradle her, and he and Stephanie watch over her.

📹 *Picture story*

INDIVIDUAL SIGNS OF THE START OF DISTRESS: POSSETTING

Emily D, 2 weeks

Signs that the baby is starting to become distressed or feel overloaded by stimulation can range from obvious behaviour like crying, to more subtle cues. These include turning away from the stimulation, yawning, grimacing and back-arching. But in some babies they can also include possetting. Emily's mother, Siobhan, describes Emily as a quiet baby who rarely shows her distress in obvious ways like crying. However, Siobhan has noticed that Emily tends to posset a little milk when she has been exposed to a great deal of stimulation. These possets are not associated with recent feeding, but rather with a need for a reduction in stimulation.

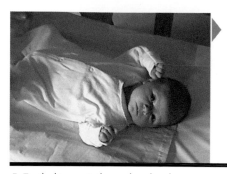

1 Emily lies quietly on her back without any apparent distress.

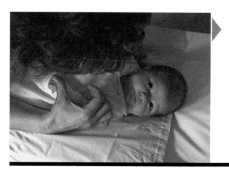

5 Emily's gaze remains averted, and Liz stops trying to attract her attention…

9 She turns a little towards Liz, still looking content…

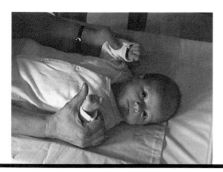

2 As Liz tries to chat and play with her, Emily keeps her eyes averted.

3 She eventually turns her head and eyes fractionally in Liz's direction, but her gaze is not full on. All the while she continues to look content.

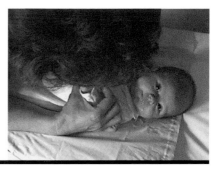

4 In the next moment, however, Emily possets some milk.

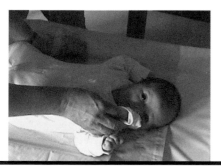

6 ...and mops up the posset.

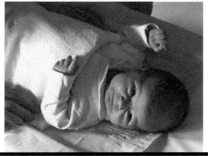

7 A little later, Liz tries to engage with her again. Emily looks firmly away...

8 ...but still shows no sign of distress.

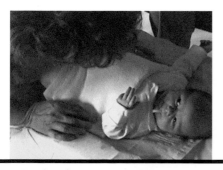

10 ...but then possets again.

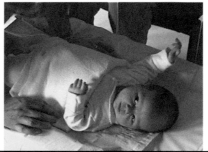

11 Together with her reluctance to look full on at Liz, her possets signal that she is not available for play.

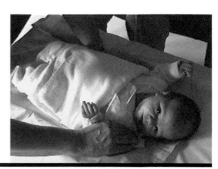

12 Liz cleans up the posset and abandons any further attempt to engage Emily in play.

📽 *Picture story*
BATHING

Natasha, 3 weeks

In the first few weeks, some babies find bath-time an overwhelmingly distressing experience, and can scream throughout. Even those who can enjoy some parts of the process find certain procedures distressing – for example when they are lowered into, or lifted from, the water. Natasha is one such baby, but her mother, Juliette, feels there is enough that is positive about the experience for her daughter to maintain bath-time as a daily routine. For babies whose distress is more extreme, however, either having the baby take her bath with a parent or else 'topping and tailing' may be appropriate until the baby is better able to cope.

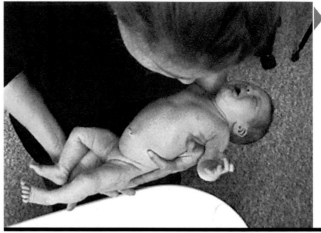

1 As Natasha is lowered towards the bath she loses the security and comfort of close contact with Juliette, and starts to show her alarm, with her arms shooting out as though to grab some support, and her back arching up.

4 This next part is, however, rather more difficult to manage and Natasha makes her objections clear.

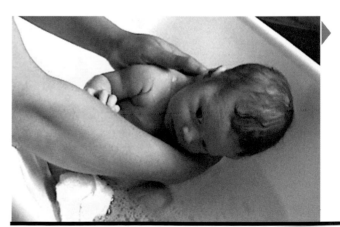

7 Now she can even stay relaxed through a change in position and the new feeling of having her back washed.

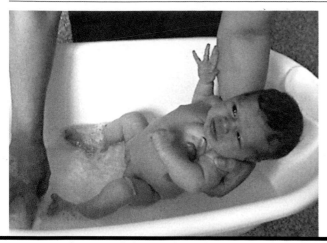

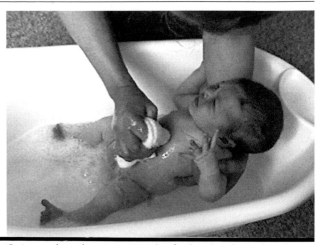

2 As Natasha is gently lowered into the warm water, the feeling of alarm seems to have abated somewhat, but she still looks tense and apprehensive, and her right hand still seems to be grasping for contact.

3 As washing begins, Natasha finds it hard to relax, but she is just about managing to tolerate the new stimulation without undue distress.

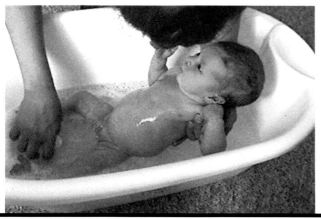

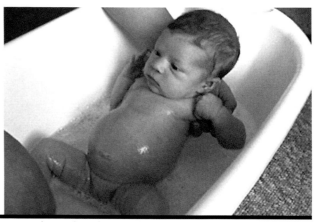

5 Now the new stimulation has stopped and Natasha is more used to being in the water, she can start to relax. Her arms now curl in and she is even able to start taking in her environment, and look up to her mother's face.

6 A calm, rather dreamy time is had now. Natasha is fully relaxed and enjoys the simple experience of the warm water around her.

8 Natasha is calm and alert as Juliette makes preparations to take her out of the bath.

continues over the page

📽 *Picture story*

BATHING

continued from previous page

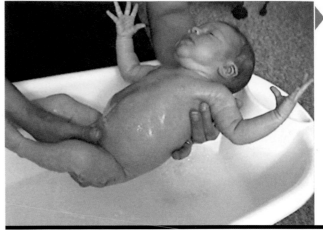

9 Although she is perfectly safe as Juliette lifts her, leaving the warmth and enclosed space of the bath tub is a shock, and Natasha's arms shoot out wildly.

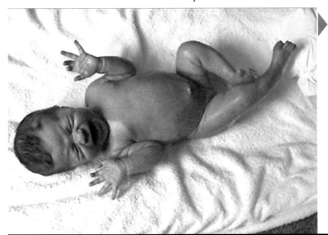

12 ...and becomes really distressed.

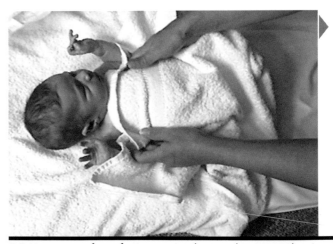

15 Her sense of comfort grows as the towel is secured around her, and her arms are contained.

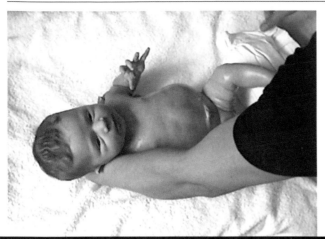

10 With Juliette's arm around her as she is placed on the towel, Natasha starts to settle.

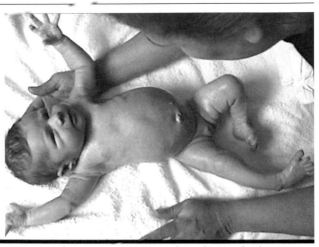

11 But as the support is removed, and Natasha lies uncovered flat on her back she begins to feel alarmed once more...

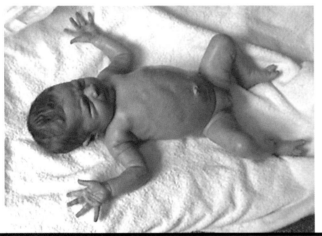

13 The most difficult moment is over, but Natasha grimaces and her wide-stretched arms show she is still experiencing some difficulty.

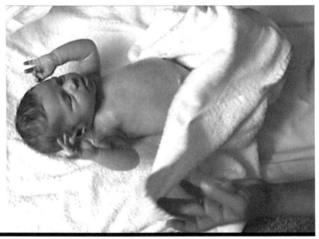

14 It is not until she feels the security of the towel covering her body that Natasha starts to relax.

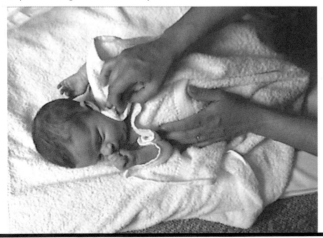

16 She can now bring her thumb up for a suck...

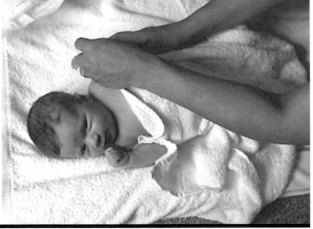

17 ...and feeling restored and secure, she is ready to look up to her mother's face and engage with her.

🎥 *Picture story*
AVOIDING DIFFICULT SITUATIONS

Isabelle, 1 week

Isabelle finds being undressed distressing, and quickly starts to flail around. Liz suggests a technique that may help prevent this situation developing. On this occasion, as she prepares Isabelle for a nappy change, she removes only the minimum of clothing, and she ensures that Isabelle's arms cannot shoot out by securing them in the baby-gro. In this position Isabelle also has easy access to her fists, should she need to suck on them.

1 Isabelle lies quietly, her body and arms amply covered, as Liz begins to roll up the lower part of Isabelle's baby-gro.

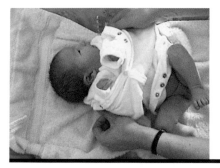

5 ...she tucks the loose edges of the baby-gro firmly under Isabelle...

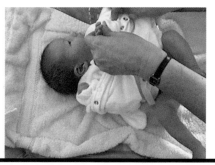

6 ...and moves Isabelle's left arm so that her fist is easily accessible for sucking.

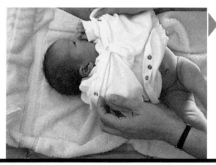

7

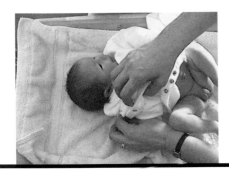

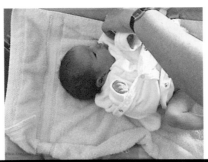

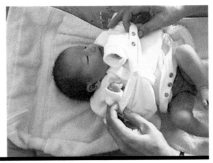

2 Liz tucks Isabelle's right arm into the baby-gro...

3 ...and then does the same thing with her left arm.

4 Liz pulls the baby-gro up a little further, so that Isabelle's arms are securely contained...

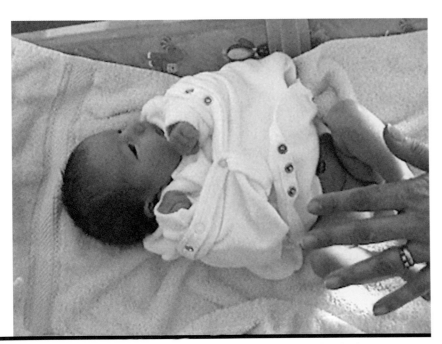

8 In fact, Isabelle feels no need to suck, and is free instead to look up at Liz and engage with her.

🎥 *Picture story*

REDUCING DISTRESS WITH THE SECURITY OF A COVER

Emily D, 1 week

Some babies, particularly in the first few weeks, find being undressed and having their nappy changed distressing. A blanket, soft towel or sheet can be used to cover the baby partially, while the nappy is being changed. This can make the baby feel less vulnerable.

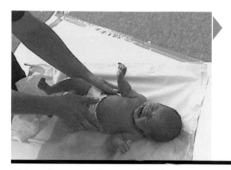

1 Liz places Emily on a blanket to prepare her for a nappy change. Even being placed on her back when she is partially undressed causes her to cry.

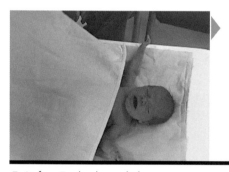

5 At first Emily shows little response, and her eyes remain shut.

'TOPPING AND TAILING'

Jake, 1 week

Jake has found bath-times very difficult. For the time being, until he is more settled, Sarah is washing him in stages, removing only one part of his clothing at a time. Jake finds even some of these mild intrusions uncomfortable, but it is a lot less traumatic than being fully undressed and bathed.

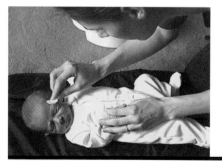

1 Jake winces and turns away as Sarah washes his face, containing one arm with her hand.

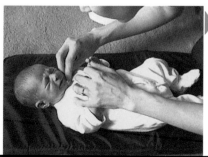

2 He screws up his eyes and resists as his mother progresses to his chin, but with her support he manages not to 'fall apart'.

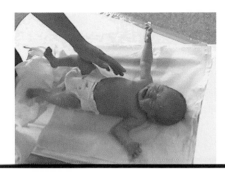

2 This intensifies as Liz removes the support of her hands, and Emily's arms fly out in her alarm.

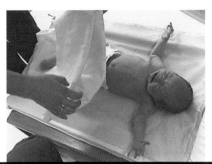

3 Liz gets a soft sheet as Emily continues to cry...

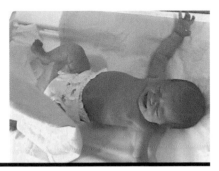

4 ...and begins to place it over her body.

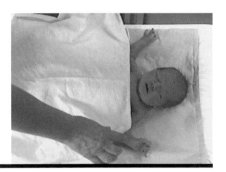

6 As the cover is tucked around her, Emily's arms begin to relax, the crying abates, and her eyes begin to open.

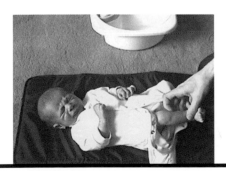

3 Jake finds the initial removal of his baby-gro from his legs unpleasant.

4 But he adjusts, and is even able to focus on what is going on around him.

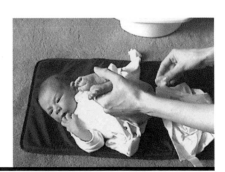

5 Looking around, and comforting himself with his fingers, Jake seems almost unaware of the manoeuvres to wash his bottom.

HELPING THE BABY CALM HERSELF
Various soothing techniques

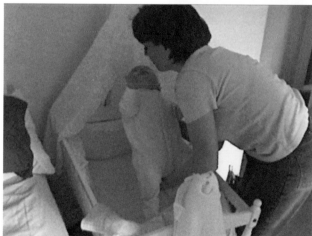

As well as being alert to those situations that provoke distress, it is also useful for parents to notice whether the baby has the ability to calm herself. Helping the baby to find and use her own resources to manage her state, even in small ways in the early weeks, will stand her in good stead in the longer term. Some babies, for example, find sucking on their fists to be soothing, but finding their fist may not always be easy. In such cases, the parent may be able to help the baby by positioning her in such a way that her fists are close to her mouth, so that she can easily soothe herself. Other babies seem to find it calming to watch something, like a patterned surface, and if this is placed within the baby's visual range, she will have the opportunity of looking at it to calm herself.

SOOTHING TECHNIQUES

Some babies require very little assistance to calm themselves if they have started to become upset, and just the sound of a familiar voice can help. Other sounds, too, can be effective, such as a simple, rhythmical lullaby, or even steady, low-level domestic noises like a tumble drier. Most babies, however, need more active support if they have already started to cry. If the baby is distressed because she is tired, then continuous rhythmic rocking in a horizontal position is likely to help. Rocking more intermittently in an upright position is likely to be more effective for a baby who is distressed but wide awake. (It is important to be aware, however, that rocking that is really vigorous may be dangerous for the baby, and could have the same effect on the brain as shaking). Some babies may respond only with a combination of several kinds of support, as in rocking the baby securely and singing to her at the same time.

It does not always follow, however, that the more input there is, the more successfully the baby will calm. Some babies, and especially those who are sensitive, become easily overloaded by stimulation, even if it was enjoyable a short while previously, and they will respond better if stimulation is reduced, and the parent takes them into a quiet, semi-darkened room. Such babies may cry or fret for a short time before they settle, but they will be able to do so more quickly in the absence of stimulation than when held and rocked.

As the baby develops, the strategies parents use for coping with infant crying also tend to change. From three months, if daily routines like feeding, bedtime procedures and nappy changes have become predictable to the baby, she will be better able to anticipate what will happen next. This will help her to cope better with situations she previously found difficult, and will begin to be able to tolerate short delays in her parents' response. By adjusting the timing of their responses in accordance with the baby's ability to tolerate delay, and giving the baby experience of a predictable, reliable structure to daily routines, parents are also effectively helping the baby to develop her own resources to cope with the inevitable ups and downs of family life.

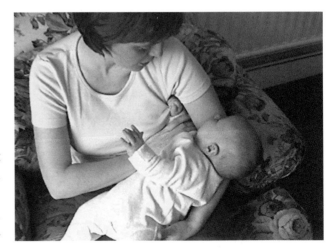

📽 *Picture story*

DISTRESS AND SELF-SOOTHING

Isabelle, 1 week

Isabelle finds each stage of being undressed for a nappy change or bath distressing, but she has good resources for calming herself, being adept at finding her thumb and sucking on it.

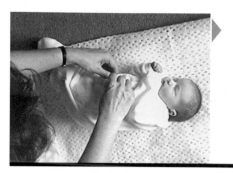

1 Preparations for bath-time begin.

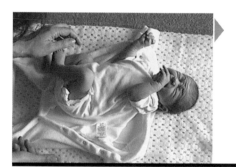

5 Isabelle brings her left hand up to her mouth, and she starts to suck.

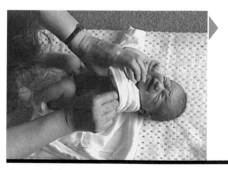

9 ...and then starts to cry.

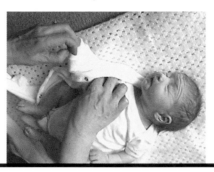

2 As Isabelle's baby-gro is removed, her arms shoot out...

3 ...she frowns and grimaces...

4 ...and becomes really distressed.

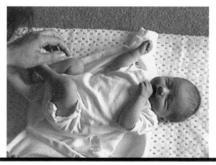

6 Her distress subsides and she becomes calm...

7 ...until the next manoeuvre – again her arm shoots out.

8 Isabelle grimaces and frowns...

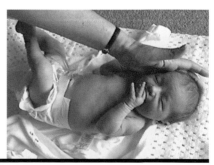

10 Her distress escalates as her body is exposed.

11 Isabelle flails around, her crying unabated...

12 ...but then she manages to find her thumb, and once again rapidly soothes herself as she sucks.

■■ *Picture story*

HELPING THE BABY CALM HERSELF

Alex, 1 week

Babies who find sucking on their fist soothing can be helped in the early weeks by securing their arms so that their fist is easily accessible.

1 Alex is distressed, and Catherine has wrapped him so that his fists are secured near his mouth.

2 Alex seems to try to devour his fist, so desperate is he to suck.

REDUCING STIMULATION

Ethan, 11 weeks

Sometimes it can seem as though nothing the parent does to try to calm a fretful baby works, and the more active their input, like rocking or singing, the more distressed the baby becomes. In these circumstances it can be helpful to cut stimulation down, for example by taking the baby to a quiet, dimly-lit room for a few minutes.

1 Ethan has had a busy morning, with the stimulation of several visitors. Now he is fractious.

5 ...she takes him upstairs.

3 The magic works, Alex gains great comfort from sucking, and his furrowed brow is smoothed...

4 ...and he continues to suck away in earnest.

6 Feeling restored, Alex can engage with the world around him once more.

2 Julie tries rocking him and singing to him, but Ethan does not respond at all.

3 Carrying him up at her shoulder and walking around doesn't seem to help either.

4 Julie decides that Ethan is finding stimulation difficult to manage, so...

6 Having drawn the curtains so that the room is dim, Julie sits quietly with Ethan, but his gaze locks on to her face, and he remains agitated.

7 Julie feels that Ethan needs to be free of all distraction, including social contact...

8 ...she puts him into the familiar environment of his cot, and he finally begins to calm.

📷 *Picture story*

THE CALMING EFFECT OF A GOOD BOOK!

Ethan, 11 weeks

Some babies can at times be helped to settle and become calm by visual stimulation. Designs that babies find attractive early on are patterns with strong, clear contrasts.

Ethan is rather fractious, but he doesn't seem to want to feed, sleep or play face-to-face games. Julie sits down with Ethan and shows him a book with a variety of black and white patterns. Ethan quickly becomes absorbed in them and he calms.

1 Ethan is fretful and Julie decides to try having a quiet time with him, sitting down with a picture book.

4 Held securely by his mother, Ethan becomes animated, and is quickly absorbed by the high contrast patterns.

8 Each of the patterns fascinates Ethan.

For details of how and where to purchase this black and white book, see p.176

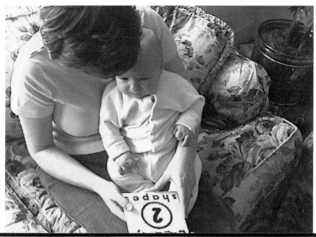

2 In the first instance, Ethan doesn't seem sure, as he continues to whimper and frown.

3 However, even the book cover soon attracts his interest, and he begins to settle.

5 He concentrates intently as his mother turns the pages. She gives him plenty of time to examine each pattern...

6 ...before moving on to the next one, and supports his looking with occasional, gently-spoken comments.

9 He begins to explore the book with his fingers.

10 A difficult time has been turned around by Julie's sensitive support of Ethan's natural interest and pleasure in visual patterns.

📽 *Picture story*

HORIZONTAL ROCKING AND CUDDLING

Natasha, 3 weeks, with her grandmother

For a baby who finds it difficult to go off to sleep without having active physical contact, horizontal rocking and cuddling can be effective in helping the baby to calm down and settle.

1 Natasha is tired, and in a distressed state, and she is finding it hard to go off to sleep.

5

VERTICAL ROCKING AND CUDDLING

Emily D, 2 weeks

A baby who is fretful, but who is not tired, can be helped by vertical rocking or cuddling. Once settled up on a shoulder, with fists easily accessible, the baby may be calm and fully alert, and enjoy looking around.

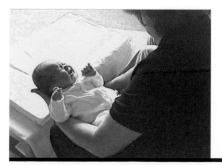

1 Although she is not tired, Emily is distressed and fretful – and she is not in a state to enjoy a face-to-face interaction.

2 Liz lifts Emily...

2 Her grandmother contains her firmly in her arms, holding Natasha horizontally.

3 Natasha's grandmother rocks her from side to side, and her distress gradually subsides.

4

6 Natasha is now calm and drowsy...

7 ...and she falls asleep.

3 ...and rocks her gently up and down on her shoulder. Emily is still distressed, but finds her fist and sucks.

4 Emily has calmed, and sucks contentedly.

5 Now she can begin to take in the world around her. She becomes alert and watches nearby events with interest.

Picture story

BECOMING FAMILIAR WITH ROUTINES HELPS THE BABY TO ANTICIPATE, TAKE PART, AND TOLERATE DELAY 1

Parents often establish routine ways of doing things with their baby, particularly with events like feeding or nappy-changing that are repeated several times a day. These routines may seem simple, but they involve subtle, minute adjustments that are unique to the individual concerned. Over the weeks, as the baby receives care that is consistent and reliable, she will become familiar with the sequence of events, and she will increasingly be able to anticipate what is coming next and play her own part more actively, as well as being better able to tolerate minor delays.

Emily D, 7 weeks

By now, Emily has become familiar with her mother's routines for feeding her. This enables her to anticipate when a feed is coming. However, it is still difficult for her to take an active part in the process, and particularly difficult for her to tolerate any delay once preparations are clearly under way.

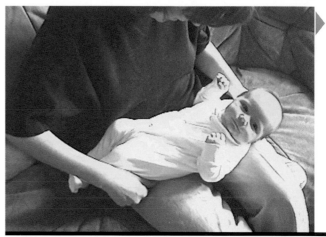

1 Emily wants to feed, so Siobhan settles on the sofa where day-time feeds usually take place.

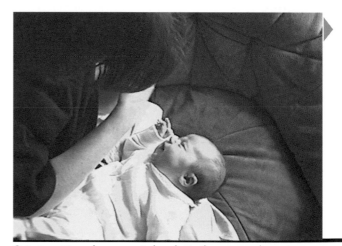

3 Just waiting, however is hard; Emily starts to become agitated...

5 Emily's ability to take an active part in getting the feed under way is still limited; she turns her head in readiness, but she still has to rely on her mother to position her...

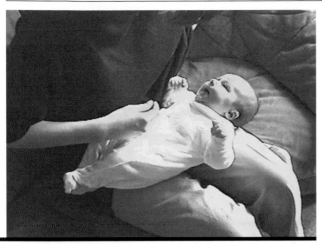

2 As Siobhan prepares to feed, Emily becomes excited; she has picked up quickly the cues that something important is about to happen.

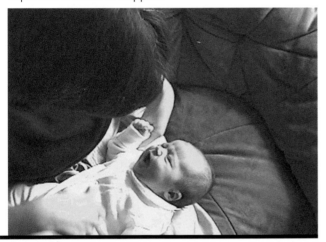

4 ...and begins to cry.

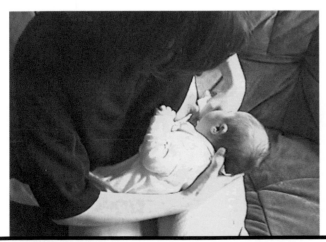

6 ...and as Siobhan supports her head, Emily turns more actively towards the breast and reaches up with her hand.

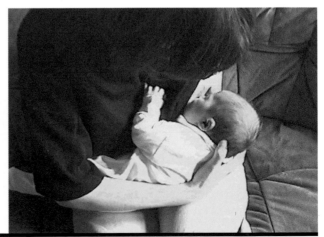

7 Soon she is comfortably settled into a feed.

🎥 *Picture story*

BECOMING FAMILIAR WITH ROUTINES HELPS THE BABY TO ANTICIPATE, TAKE PART, AND TOLERATE DELAY 2

Ethan, 11 weeks

Ethan is almost three months old. By now he is very used to Julie's way of getting ready for a feed; he is able to use these cues to prepare himself, and can wait without becoming distressed.

1 Ethan is hungry, so Julie takes him over to the chair she normally uses for feeds. Over the weeks they have evolved their own, unique, preparations.

4 Ethan knows the routine well, and now he calms and waits as Julie makes the initial adjustments to her clothing.

7 ...and twists his body into position, using his hand as well to get access to the nipple...

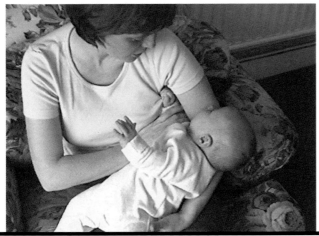

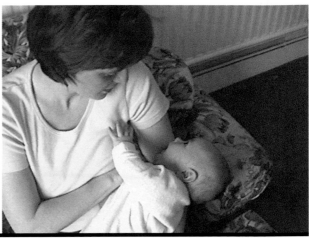

2 Having settled comfortably in the chair, and positioned Ethan on her lap, Julie tucks Ethan's hand under her arm.

3 This is Ethan's cue that a feed is on its way, and he immediately signals his excitement, looking up at Julie expectantly, and starting to kick his legs.

5 As Julie's preparations progress, Ethan starts to position himself in readiness: he tilts his head, adjusts his posture and...

6 ...starts to open his mouth, and lifts his hand...

8 ...and the feed is under way.

LONGER-TERM DEVELOPMENT AND SUPPORT FOR PARENTS

The importance of meeting babies' and parents' needs

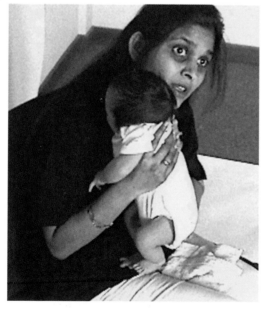

Although patterns of parental care are not obviously related to how much a baby cries in the first few weeks, the way in which parents initially respond to their baby's crying affects how much that baby will cry or is able to soothe herself when she is one year old. When parents are able to tune in early to their baby's experience and communication, and respond with whatever strategy the individual infant requires to reduce her distress, the baby is likely to cry less later on. This even applies to babies who are more sensitive than others and who cry persistently in the early weeks. Giving care that is sensitive to the baby's unique signals, which is reliable and predictably structured, will help the baby to build up a sense of a familiar world in which events can be anticipated, and in which minor delays and difficulties can be more easily tolerated.

The kind of care that babies need is more easily given if the parents themselves are well supported. If there is no-one to sympathise and help, having a baby who cries a great deal, and who is highly sensitive, can leave parents feeling demoralised and depressed. It is important that parents do not feel they ought to struggle on without assistance. Asking a relative or friend to take on some of the demands of the household such as shopping, organising washing, cooking meals – in short, to help care for the parents themselves – is absolutely appropriate. Some parents may also feel they would like someone they trust to take the baby for a while so that they can have a break and replenish their resources. With regard to further support in managing the crying itself, if health care professionals like the Health Visitor or GP have not been able to give sufficient help, it is worth thinking of contacting self-help groups with crying as a special focus, like the Cry-sis Helpline (tel 020 7404 5011).

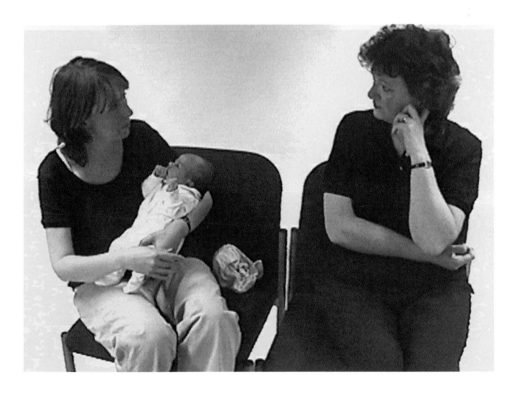

CHAPTER FOUR

SLEEPING

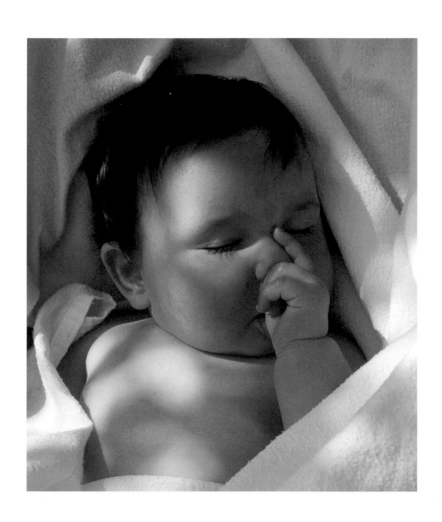

HOW MUCH DO BABIES SLEEP?

And variations in the patterns

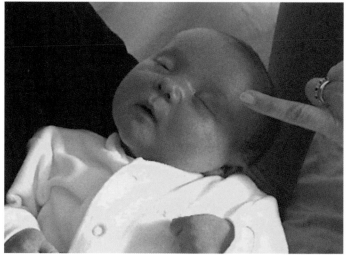

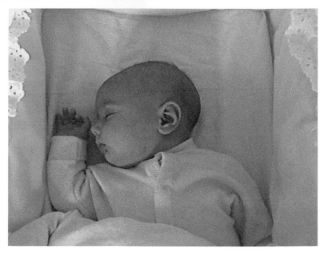

In the first few weeks following birth, babies spend around 15-16 hours asleep each day, but by three months this has gradually dropped to about 14 hours. These are, however, only average times, and how much a baby sleeps can vary quite a lot from one day to the next, often depending on whether or not the baby is taken out, as well as on how much is going on at home. There are also marked individual differences between babies in the amount they sleep, some seeming to need far less, or far more, than others. Whether your baby is one who sleeps less or more than average is generally clear by about six weeks. These differences generally persist, with the overall amount of time that individual babies tend to sleep remaining fairly stable throughout the first year. In this respect sleep is quite unlike crying, where individual patterns can change dramatically after the first few months.

SLEEP CYCLES

Although the overall tendency of each baby to sleep less or more than others is relatively stable, the timing of the baby's sleep changes a great deal as the weeks go by. Even before birth, babies show distinct periods of rest and activity, and these generally show some regularity in terms of the time of day when the different phases of the cycle occur. To some extent this pattern carries over into the newborn period, especially in the timing of quiet periods, so that at first the baby is no more likely to sleep at night than during the day-time. The longest period spent asleep by newborns and babies in the first two weeks is usually about four hours, but by three months this has, on average, increased to between six and eight hours, and by then these long periods generally occur at night-time.

Over time, the quality of sleep changes too. Newborn babies start off their sleep cycles in what is called 'REM' sleep, and up to half their sleep is in this state. REM sleep refers to Rapid Eye Movements, which can be detected through the eyelids as fluttering movements that come in bursts. These eye movements are often accompanied by irregular breathing, and jerks or twitches of the limbs.

As well as these periods of rapid eye movement sleep, babies' sleep can be divided into phases of light and deep sleep. The proportion of sleep that is deep increases over the first few weeks, and both babies and children sleep much more in this state than do adults. In deep sleep babies are less easily aroused than in light sleep, their breathing is more steady and regular, and there is little movement. Throughout the time when the baby is sleeping, these different states of deep and light sleep occur in cycles. A whole cycle usually lasts a little under an hour and it is regularly interspersed with periods of arousal which may last from a few seconds to several minutes. At times, arousals are spontaneous, when the baby begins to move around and shift towards an awake state, but sometimes the baby is aroused from light sleep by her own movements, if they are violent or jerky, or by things that are going on around her.

How easily the individual baby is aroused from sleep can help parents think about the arrangements they want to make for where they put the baby to sleep. For a baby who goes off to sleep easily, and who sleeps very soundly, the place where the baby has a day-time nap will not matter too much, but for one who is easily woken from sleep, parents may want to find somewhere where disturbance is likely to be minimal.

📽 *Picture story*

SHUTTING OUT DISTURBING NOISES *Emily D, 7 weeks*

Some babies are able to adjust to a repeated noise, and can
shut it out and remain asleep when the noise recurs.

1 Emily is asleep.

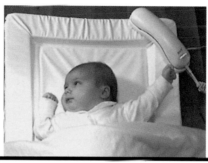

2 As soon as the phone rings she wakes with a large startle.

3 As the noise continues, Emily tries to shut it out...

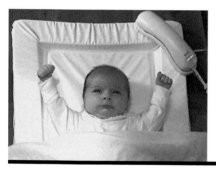

7 ...once again her eyes open...

8 ...and she becomes upset.

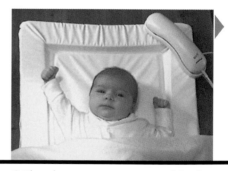

9 The phone stops ringing and Emily relaxes...

13

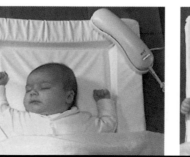

14 The phone rings again. This time it does not wake her immediately.

15 Although she is briefly aroused, she does not startle or become distressed...

Emily is particularly robust during sleep, and she copes well with the intrusion of everyday noises such as the telephone ringing. This means that her parents do not have to take special steps to adjust Emily's environment to enable her to settle to sleep soundly.

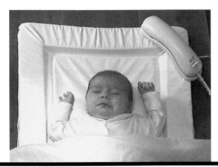

4 ...but it still disturbs her...

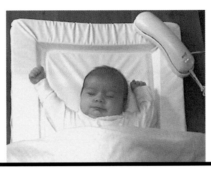

5 ...and she frowns, grimaces and shifts about until...

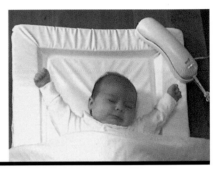

6

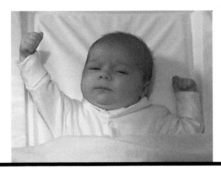

10 ...and gradually slips back to sleep on her own...

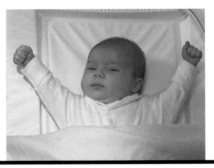

11 ...requiring no additional assistance from her parents.

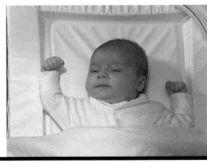

12

16 ...and as the sound continues, Emily is able to shut it out...

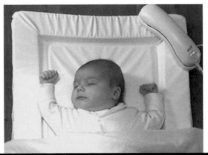

17 ...and slip back into a sound sleep.

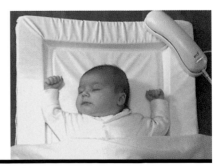

18

WHERE AND WHEN BABIES SLEEP
Matching up babies' characteristics with parental preference and lifestyles

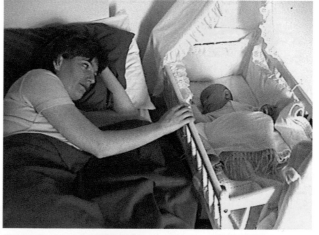

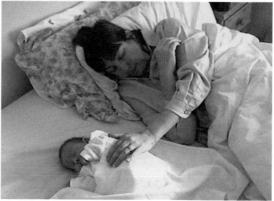

WHERE BABIES SLEEP

There are big differences between cultures in how parents view sleeping arrangements. In some cultures, particularly where closeness to the baby is highly valued, and the child's independence is not a big issue, parents and their babies sleep together, and this can continue over a number of years. This applies not only to cultures that are non-industrialised – the Japanese, for example, typically practise bed-sharing with their infants and young children. In the UK, by contrast, parents generally want different arrangements, and most aim to have their baby sleep on her own through the night by the time the baby is six months old. There is, however, variation within cultures, and some parents in Britain put a lower value on sleeping separately.

In the early weeks after your baby's birth, it is worth thinking through your beliefs and values on this issue, for babies' sleeping habits start to become established within the first three months. If you are parents who feel that it is important to you to have your baby sleep on her own without interrupting you during the night, then adopting particular strategies over the first few months, as your baby becomes ready, will increase your chances of achieving this pattern. How you eventually settle for one strategy rather than another is, however, also likely to be influenced by your baby's individual characteristics. Some babies find it much harder than others to go off to sleep without quite a lot of active support, and you may decide that, in spite of your initial feelings that bed-sharing is not your preferred option, it is the route that offers the best solution, given your baby's characteristics and the other demands on you. After all, babies probably slept with their parent for warmth and security during most of the time that our species was evolving. (See section on co-sleeping, p.161.)

ESTABLISHING THE DAY AND NIGHT DIFFERENCE

Each baby is born with her own unique rhythms of quiet and active states, and each family has its own rhythms. Gradually, the baby and her parents become synchronised, but at the outset they are quite disparate, and the way they become adjusted to each other around the clock takes time, and will involve a unique set of exchanges and adaptations between them. Where there is a fairly stable pattern of living in the household, interactions between parents and their baby take place quite naturally in the course of ordinary daily routines that will help the baby to adapt to the parents' own rhythms and day-night cycle. For example, feeds that take place in the morning are likely to be carried out in an entirely different atmosphere from those occurring in the middle of the night.

In the morning there may be noises and activity around the home, bright lights, the presence of siblings. Even in the first few days, parents can engage with the baby in a social way that maintains the baby's alert state. For example, a feed may be followed by a nappy change, which, with a baby who is not distressed by the procedure, can be a prime opportunity for social engagement. This might, for example, be followed by the mother carrying the baby against her shoulder while she gets herself a drink, an upright position that typically helps the baby to be alert.

A feed in the middle of the night, on the other hand, is likely to be an entirely different experience for the baby. The home is likely to be hushed and in darkness, and social contacts and other activity are likely to be markedly reduced. Having the baby sleep near the parents, for example, in a crib alongside the parents' bed, gives both the baby and parents repeated opportunities through the night to sense each others' rhythms through changing breathing patterns and state. Daily repeated experiences of this kind naturally entrain the baby into the parents' lifestyle. This entrainment is best done in the context of the baby's own cycles of sleep, wakefulness and feeding. Thus, babies who are woken to be fed, thereby breaking into their natural cycle, are likely to have their behaviour and sleep pattern disrupted.

SETTLING THE BABY TO SLEEP

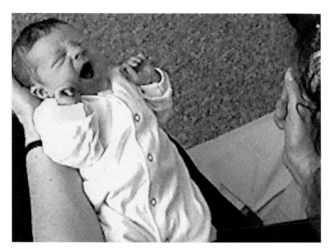

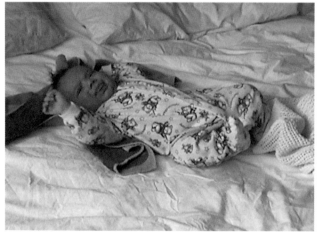

Some babies can fall asleep anywhere, and can move smoothly from waking to sleeping without active support. Others find these transitions much more stressful, and are helped by particular kinds of environment. Close observation of your own baby's behaviour during these transitions can be valuable in developing strategies that, in the long run, will make for a less stressful time for both the parents and the baby.

It is particularly helpful to notice the individual baby's cues and behaviour as she begins to become tired. Some babies start, for example, to turn away and avoid stimulation. Others may become agitated, fussy or irritable. Others may simply become drowsy as they gaze at their surroundings. Watching the individual way in which your baby behaves as she is becoming tired will help you know when to begin preparations for assisting your baby through the transition to sleep. If the parent consistently links the routine the family has for settling the baby to these signs that she is tiring, the baby will be able to use that routine in the future as a cue for settling down to sleep.

POSSIBLE USEFUL STRATEGIES

In the first few weeks it is typical for babies to be put down in their cot or crib when they are already asleep. By about three months, however, most babies are put down in the place where they are to sleep when they are still awake. As is explained later, this is relevant to helping your baby sleep through the night, and we have therefore outlined some strategies below that might be used to assist your baby to make the transition from being awake to falling asleep.

As mentioned, babies vary widely in what will help them shift to a sleep state, and a number of strategies are described, from those for babies who find it relatively easy to settle, to those for babies who experience much more difficulty. In highlighting these strategies, consideration has been given to the fact that many parents will want to find a method to help their infant settle which, in the long term, will not involve them in having to give direct physical support to the baby themselves (for example, by rocking the baby in their arms, or patting her in her cot, or feeding her), especially during the night. Rather, parents may wish to help their baby develop her own strategies, so that she is content to go off to sleep on her own. For other parents this will not be an issue, and they may feel entirely comfortable about the prospect of being in close contact with their baby as she falls asleep.

1. USING SIGHTS AND SOUNDS

Some babies need relatively little direct support from their parent, and are calmed by, for example, simply watching things around them. If the parents have noticed that this is the case, they may subsequently, as soon as they notice the first sign that the baby is getting tired, lay her on her back in her crib or cot with some attractive pattern within view. A mobile securely placed within the baby's range of focus may serve well, especially if it has distinct visual contrasts and edges; or a patterned surface along the side of the cot may engross the baby and help to soothe her off to sleep. Other similarly easily settled babies benefit from an auditory stimulus – a music tape, for example, played as the baby is placed in her cot.

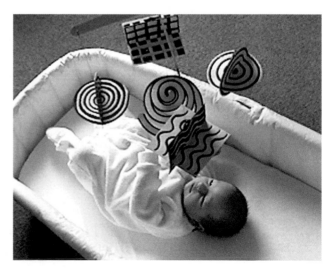

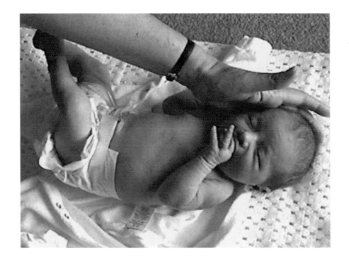

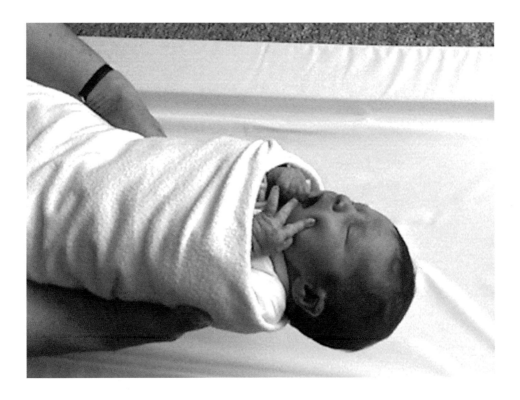

2. USING SUCKING

Other babies require more active stimulation through physical contact to help them go to sleep. Many young babies, for example, find sucking very soothing. This can be confusing for mothers who are breast-feeding 'on demand', for they may easily misinterpret the baby's cues and imagine that the baby is actually hungry. The mother in this situation may well offer the breast, and indeed the baby may suck, become less distressed, and fall asleep. The potential difficulty with establishing this pattern is that the baby will become adjusted to it, and may subsequently find it difficult to go off to sleep without sucking at the breast. Some families do not find this at all problematic, and will be quite happy to develop this pattern as their normal routine. Others, however, will wish to avoid setting up this kind of pattern. In such cases it is helpful to think about how the baby's tendency to find sucking soothing can be supported in other ways, having checked first, of course, to see whether or not the baby really *is* hungry.

As parents become experienced in feeding the baby, they will begin to be able to distinguish different qualities in the baby's manner of sucking. Then, if the baby neither roots, nor sucks strongly when offered the parent's finger, as she does when she is really hungry, then helping her simply to comfort suck, rather than feeding her, may give her the support she needs to make the transition to sleep. Some babies who find sucking helpful are comforted by sucking on their fist. Some can achieve this on their own, and can simply be placed in their cot as they become tired and left without any special strategy to support sucking. Others can find their fist in the early weeks only when they are wrapped in such a way that their fist is positioned near their mouth. If the baby cannot manage this kind of self control, and sucking seems to be an important way in which the baby regulates her state and calms herself to sleep, then the parents might want to consider using a dummy or pacifier to help her.

3. USING SWADDLING

Some babies require more direct physical support to make the transition to sleep. For example, some easily startle themselves out of a drowsy state with jerky arm movements. Until a few years ago, parents were encouraged to put their babies to sleep on their fronts, and it was undoubtedly the case that, for this sort of baby, the problems of these jerky movements were avoided, and the baby would be able to go soundly off to sleep without interruption. Unfortunately, the practice of placing babies to sleep in this way is now known to add to the risk of cot death, and indeed, since the campaign to put babies 'back to sleep', the number of cot deaths has been halved. For this reason, placing babies to sleep on their front is now not an option that parents can risk.

There are, however, alternatives that serve the same purpose of keeping the baby settled, even though they may seem to be more complicated. Swaddling, in which the baby's arms are gently contained, and therefore unlikely to jerk around and arouse the baby, is an age-old custom that can be very effective. As with laying a baby on her front, however, it is important that the baby does not become too hot with swaddling, and therefore a number of checks should be made. First, it is advisable to use a thin cotton sheet, rather than a blanket. The parent should also check that the baby is not overdressed, and that other covers for the baby are no more than required, given the room temperature. Finally, it is important that the baby's head is not covered. Swaddled babies, as with other babies, should ideally be placed to sleep on their back. However, if the baby seems unable to settle, then placing her on her side may be helpful. In this case the baby will need to have her lower arm positioned in front of her to prevent her rolling onto her front – bolsters or other props should not be used, as they may cause the baby's body temperature to rise.

📽 *Picture story*

BECOMING FAMILIAR WITH DIFFERENT ROOTING AND SUCKING BEHAVIOURS

Isabelle, 1 week

Parents are often confused about whether their baby is hungry, or perhaps wants to suck for comfort. Observing the baby's behaviour both when she has just had a feed (and is therefore not hungry) and when a feed is due, can help parents become aware of the significance of their baby's signals. They may then use these cues in the future to guide their decisions.

A. ABSENCE OF HUNGER

B. HUNGER

4 Her mother does the same on the other side...

5 ...and Isabelle's head-turn is swift and strong.

1 Isabelle has been fed a short while ago. Liz shows Isabelle's mother, Helen, how to check for a rooting response. A finger gently placed first on one side...

2 ...and then on the other side of Isabelle's mouth, elicits no head-turning or rooting reflex.

3 Isabelle's sucking on her mother's finger is half-hearted – Helen can sense that this is not a hungry baby.

1 Some time later, Isabelle starts to cry.

2 Now a finger placed to the side of her mouth elicits head turning,...

3 ...and Isabelle eagerly tries to take the finger in her mouth.

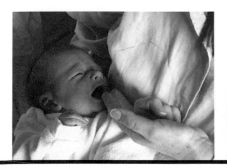

6 Isabelle opens her mouth wide to take in her mother's finger.

7 Her sucking is strong and deep, and quite different from the previous occasion.

8 Helen feels that Isabelle is hungry and ready for a feed.

🎥 *Picture story*
HOW TO SWADDLE

Natasha, 1 week

Some babies occasionally need additional support and comfort to enable them to settle down either for a rest or a sleep. This swaddling technique includes current guidelines for ensuring that a baby does not become too hot.

1 Natasha is wearing only a nappy and baby-gro. She is unsettled lying on her back, her arms are flailing, and she is unable to get her hand to her mouth to comfort suck.

SAFETY TIPS

- remove all excess clothing

- use a sheet, not a blanket

- ensure the sheet does not wrap around the baby's head

- place the baby's arms high on her chest so that she can wriggle them free

- do not place her on her front

- do not use a bolster or other prop to keep her in position

- only use additional covers if the surrounding temperature warrants it

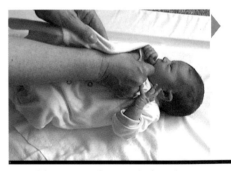

5 Holding Natasha's right hand up to her mouth, Liz begins to bring the cot sheet across Natasha's arm,...

9 The process begins again on the left side. Liz ensures that both Natasha's hands are close to her mouth.

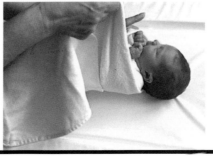

10 The other side of the cot sheet is gently and firmly wrapped around Natasha.

11

2 Liz takes a cot sheet, and folds it into a wide triangle.

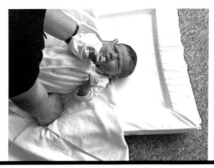

3 She carefully places Natasha onto the sheet, so that her neck is level with the top edge.

4 Since Natasha's right arm is already close to her chest, Liz starts with this, gently guiding Natasha's hand to her mouth.

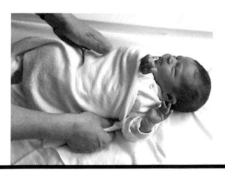

6 …and across her body.

7 Liz firmly anchors the corner of the sheet underneath Natasha.

8 Now Natasha's right arm is safely swaddled.

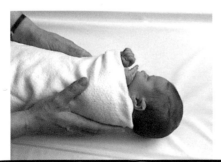

12 The corner is again secured underneath Natasha's body.

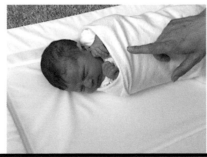

13 Natasha has enough freedom to move her hands away from her mouth…

14 …and enough support to find her hands easily again, and suck on them for comfort.

📽 *Picture story*
SWADDLING AND SLEEPING

Natasha, 3 weeks

It has been difficult for Juliette to settle Natasha to sleep in the evenings; Natasha seems to need a lot of physical support, and Juliette has been holding Natasha in her arms for up to 45 minutes each evening before she finally falls asleep. Juliette is keen to find some other less demanding solution since she is soon due to resume work, and is worried that what she can manage now just won't be possible in a few weeks' time.

Liz notes that Juliette's holding has been effective, and has provided Natasha with both frontal support and warmth. Given Juliette's imminent need to extricate herself, Liz suggests they see how Natasha responds to loose swaddling, since this provides some of the same kind of support. Indeed, this seems to work well. Within ten minutes, Natasha is sound asleep. Since Natasha has, in the past, needed such active physical support, on this occasion Liz is aware that she may have to provide some containment for Natasha with her hands, in addition to the swaddling. She also judges that it will be best to start off this new routine by positioning Natasha on her side so that she can suck her fist. Eventually, however, as Natasha adjusts to swaddling rather than being held and rocked, her mother will be able to swaddle her, and then place her to sleep on her back.

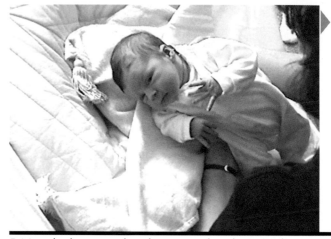

1 Natasha has started to show signs that she is tired, so Liz lifts her onto the folded sheet, in preparation for swaddling.

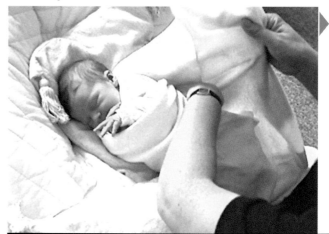

4 One side of the sheet is tucked in and the other made ready to wrap around Natasha. Meanwhile Natasha continues to suck contentedly.

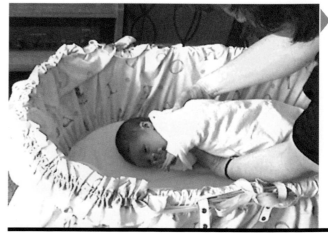

7 Natasha is still awake, and a little unsettled. Rather than move her fist away from her mouth and disturb her, Liz places Natasha, in this instance, in a position where she can continue to suck.

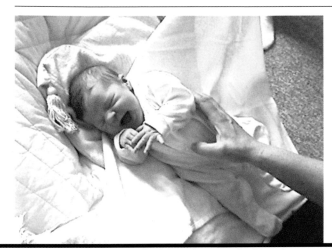

2 Natasha is becoming fretful and tries to find her fist.

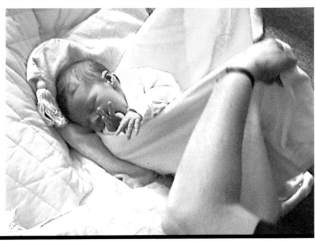

3 Liz folds the sheet so that Natasha's arm is contained, Natasha is able to find her fist, and she immediately starts sucking.

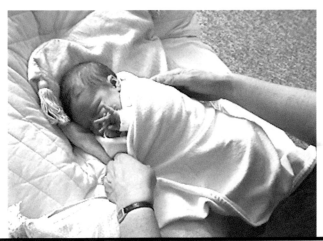

5 She is a sensitive baby and grimaces as she is moved while the sheet is wrapped around her…

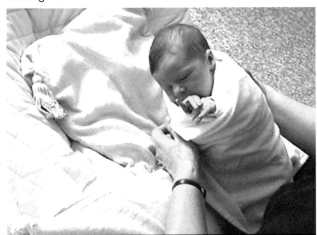

6 …but now she concentrates on sucking and calms down.

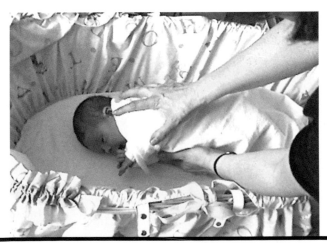

8 Knowing Natasha has previously needed a lot of support to settle, Liz keeps a firm hand on her.

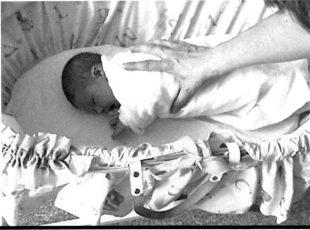

9 Gradually, it seems as though Natasha is managing to settle.

continues over the page

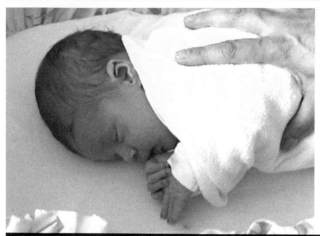

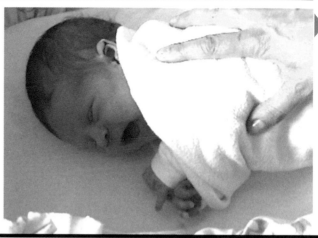

10
continued from previous page

11 But life isn't quite that simple: Natasha becomes aroused and wants to find her fist again.

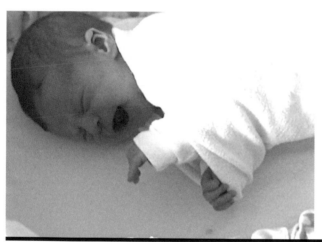

14 But Natasha remains distressed.

15

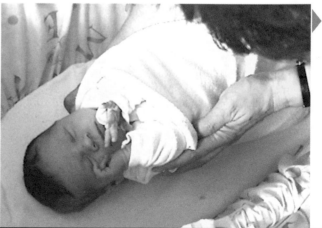

18 Natasha has finally been able to go off to sleep.

19 Since it is possible that Natasha may roll over onto her front, Liz turns her to sleep on her back…

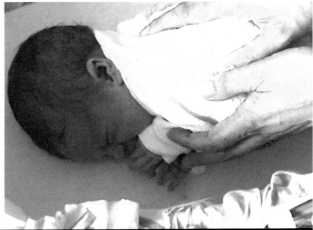

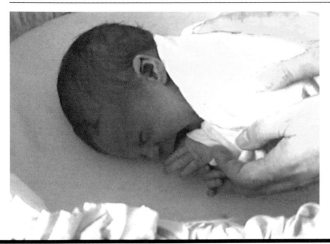

12

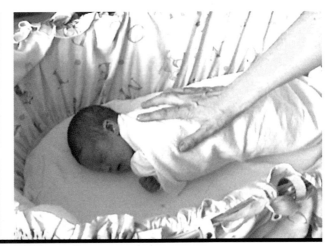

13 Liz tries to help her.

16 A hand on her back again may help Natasha feel more contained.

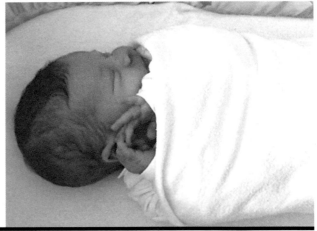

17 This really seems to help.

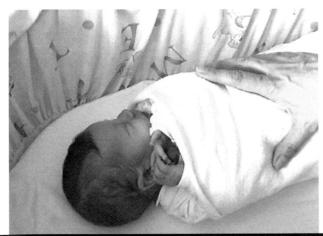

20 ...containing Natasha with her hand until the manoeuvre is complete.

21 Just ten minutes since the swaddling began, Natasha is sound asleep.

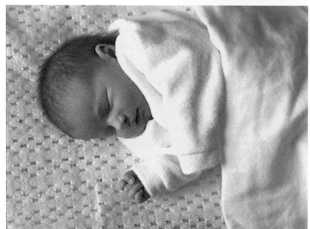

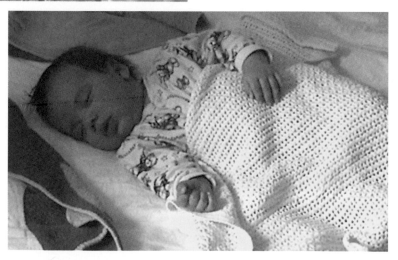

4. USING A COMBINATION OF STRATEGIES

Even with the use of the strategies already described, some babies, and particularly those whose behaviour becomes rapidly disorganised, and who become distressed when they are tired, need even more intensive support to become calm and go off to sleep. These babies are, in the first few weeks, usually highly sensitive to slight changes in their environment, and they can place great demands on their parents. Parents may be helped, however, by their greater understanding of their baby's difficulties, and in this way they may be better able to give the kind of support that the baby needs. The baby may need input from several sources of support before they can become calm, for example, by swaddling and rocking the baby at the same time.

As the weeks pass and the baby's distress reduces, she is likely gradually to develop greater capacities to manage without this high degree of parental support, and the parents will be able to adjust their care accordingly and help the baby develop her own resources without so much direct involvement themselves.

5. USING A REDUCTION IN STIMULATION

Unlike the babies described previously who seem to need active stimulation or support to make the transition to sleep, there are some who find stimulation distressing, and become even more agitated, responding better when it is cut right down. Taking these babies to a quiet, semi-darkened room, and placing them in a cot or crib, without any other stimulation may, in fact, help them to become calm enough to go off to sleep even if they are initially unsettled for a few minutes.

Some parents, possibly because of their own history of being cared for, as well as their beliefs, can find this extremely difficult. Their own feelings of panic and anguish can seem so overwhelming that they cannot quite believe that the baby will be able to manage on her own. These feelings are quite appropriate if the baby is really distressed; however, it is worth listening carefully to the baby, and trying to identify the quality of the baby's vocalisations, separately from the parent's own anxiety. If what is involved is a low-level, fretful sound that does not, in fact, have an urgency about it, and that lasts just a short time, then this strategy may, in fact, be less stressful for the baby than more active interventions.

🎥 *Picture story*

SENSITIVITY TO STIMULATION IN A TIRED BABY

Zak, 7 weeks

Zak is tired, and as a result he has become more excitable and fretful. In this state he is particularly sensitive to stimulation. He finds the changing patterns of light from the window disturbing, as well as faint background noises. Attempts to soothe him by touch are similarly distressing, and it is only when stimulation is cut right down that he is finally able to go off to sleep.

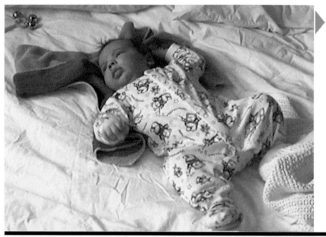

1 Zak has had a busy morning and is tired, but as he is placed on his parent's bed, he finds it difficult to settle and is drawn to look at the light filtering through the window.

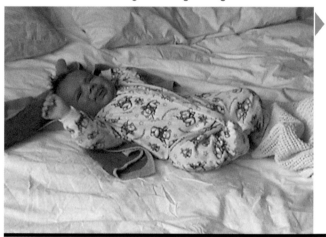

4 In spite of the discomfort it causes him, Zak is drawn back to the the light...

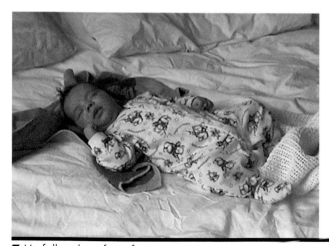

7 He falls asleep for a few moments...

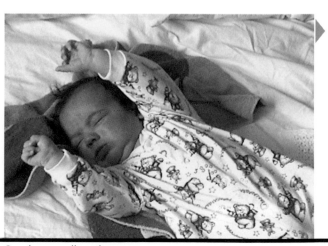

8 ...but is still restless...

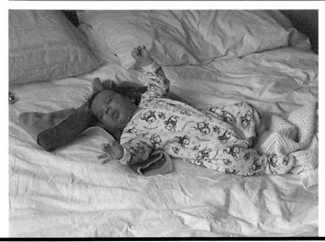

2 Transfixed by the light, Zak becomes agitated, and his arms flail around.

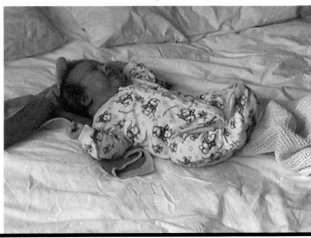

3 Eventually, he turns away, but by now he is quite fretful.

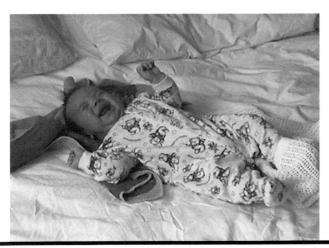

5 ...and he continues to be upset.

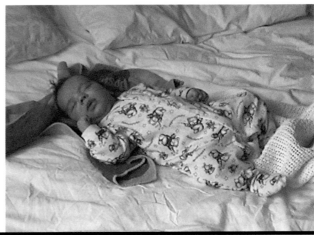

6 He starts to drift into sleep, but is easily aroused by a combination of his own 'startle' movements and the light falling on his face.

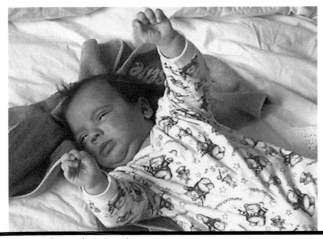

9 ...and 'startles' awake.

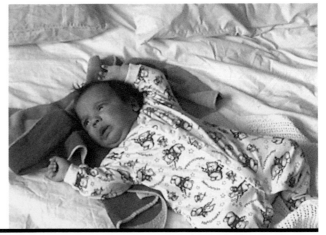

10 Zak rouses, and is once more drawn both to look at the window...

continues over the page

📽 *Picture story*

SENSITIVITY TO STIMULATION IN A TIRED BABY

continued from previous page

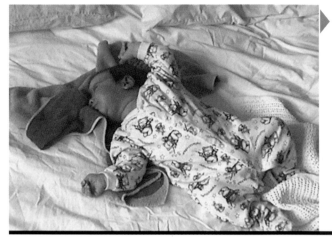

11 ...and to avoid it.

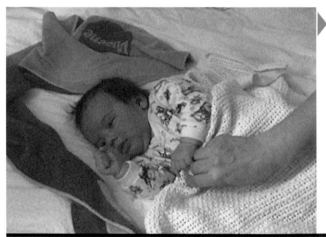

14 She also adjusts Zak's position a little so that he is no longer flat on his back and prone to flail around. Instead, his weight is shifted slightly to the side. Since his right arm is fully extended, there is no danger of him rolling on to his front.

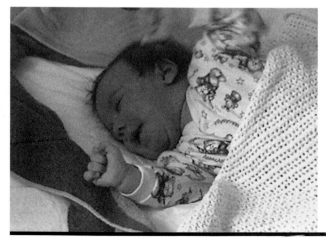

17

18 After Liz and Bina have left the room, Zak settles once again.

12 Zak's unsettled behaviour causes his mother, Bina, and Liz to approach.

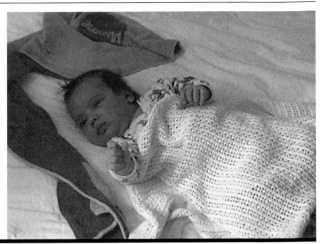

13 Liz draws the curtain.

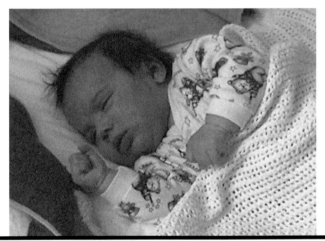

15 ...Zak shuts his eyes.

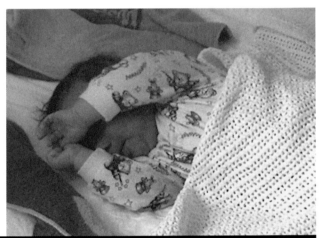

16 ...but, as Liz and Bina quietly discuss Zak's behaviour, he is unsettled by their voices.

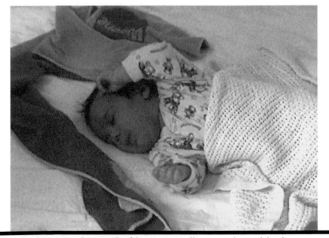

19 The muted sound of binmen collecting the rubbish outside makes Zak startle.

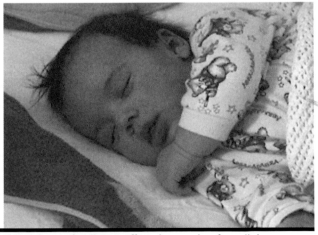

20 Zak can finally go off to sleep only after all the stimulation from light and sound has ceased.

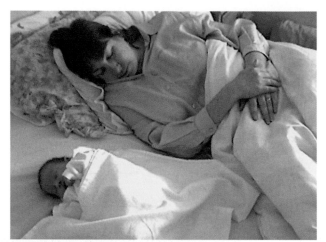

6. USING CO-SLEEPING

It is not surprising that, when the baby is one who is only easily soothed to sleep with close physical contact, parents tend to take the baby into bed with them. Indeed, as mentioned earlier, several societies practise co-sleeping as a matter of course. Recently, there have been some concerns about co-sleeping, similar to the concern about babies sleeping on their front: that is, the question of whether it poses a risk for cot death. The conclusion, however, from the research to date is that co-sleeping does not carry any significant risk, provided certain precautions are taken.

Studies of what happens during co-sleeping under recommended conditions show that parents tend to monitor the baby's position and temperature through the night, and make constant adjustments, without any conscious awareness, to enable the baby to breathe properly and to help prevent her from overheating. For example, if the baby begins to get hot and starts to change her position or move around, the parent may, quite unconsciously, lift the covers from the baby, allowing cooler air to circulate. Breast-feeding can be done during co-sleeping with minimal disruption to anyone, and in general parents do not experience their nights as being disturbed.

There may be risks to the baby, however, if the parents' ability to monitor her is impaired. For example, if the parents are excessively tired, have consumed alcohol, or taken drugs or medication that make them sleep more heavily than usual, they may not be able to fine-tune their behaviour to the baby's. Similarly, if space in the bed is limited, and the bed covers, such as duvets, are heavy, or the parents are particularly overweight, the baby may become too hot. Sleeping alongside a baby on a sofa should, in particular, be avoided. Thus, whether co-sleeping seems to be the ideal solution to the problem of an unsettled baby, or is simply the parents' preferred style of family living, it is important to ensure that it is done as safely as possible.

SAFETY TIPS

Co-sleeping has many advantages, but it is important that it is done with safety in mind, and that the following precautions are taken:

- Do not co-sleep if your responsiveness may be impaired by, for example,
  excessive tiredness
  alcohol
  drugs

- Ensure the baby cannot become too hot because, for example,
  she is over-wrapped
  the parent is very overweight and/or space is limited
  the bed covers are heavy

- Do not have pillows or bolsters near the baby

- Do not co-sleep on a sofa

🎥 *Picture sequence*

FEEDING AND SLEEPING

Emily D, 7 weeks

It is easy for a baby to fall asleep during a feed and tempting for her parents to put the baby into her cot asleep. While this may be hard to avoid in the first few weeks, if the pattern persists over the months, the baby may come to rely on being fed in order to go to sleep following night-time arousals. Unless the baby and her parents are co-sleeping, these interruptions may be difficult for the parents to sustain.

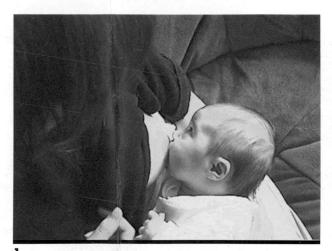

1

2

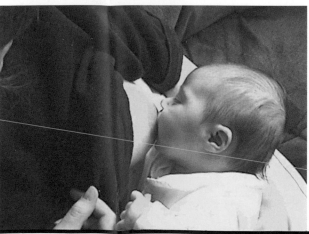

4

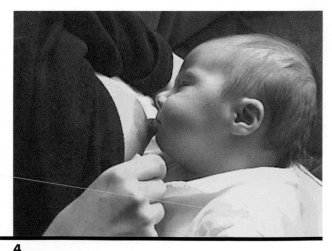

3

SLEEPING THROUGH THE NIGHT

Small babies need to wake at night to feed, but by three months about two thirds of babies are able to sleep through the night without crying (of course, there are periodic arousals, as described previously, but the baby returns to sleep on her own). Being too hot or too cold makes it difficult to sleep through the night, as does a blocked nose or cold wet nappy, or an uncomfortable position or ruck in the bed clothes. But even when none of these things occurs, some babies (around 10-15%), persist over the months in waking up and crying, possibly on several occasions through the night, and this can clearly be an exhausting, and sometimes distressing, business for the parents.

Although there are marked individual differences between babies in their tendency to sleep through the night, whether or not a baby regularly wakes and cries in the night has been found to relate to a range of parenting practices. Among these, a central issue is the way in which the baby's transitions to sleep are managed. If, by around three months, the baby either spontaneously goes off to sleep, or else can be helped to do so in some of the ways described previously, without the parent needing to be present, then the baby is more likely to be able to return to sleep on her own following her periods of night-time arousal. By contrast, if at this stage the baby's initial transition to sleep is taking place with the parent being actively involved (for example by being held in the parent's arms, or being fed, patted, or stroked to sleep), the baby is more likely to continue to need this kind of contact to resume sleep during the night. This is likely to be the reason why breast-fed babies are more prone to wake at night at three months than are bottle-fed babies – it seems not to be breast-feeding, as such, that causes the continued night-waking; but rather the fact that breast-fed babies are more often put down in their cots having fallen asleep during a feed. If breast-fed babies are put into their cots when they are starting to become drowsy, rather than when they have fallen asleep at the breast, they will have the same chance as other babies to develop the ability to manage the final transition to sleep without their mother's physical presence.

Another factor associated with persistent night-waking is birth order: first-born babies are significantly more likely to be disturbing their parents at night beyond three months than later-born children. This is likely to be due to the tendency of parents to feel uncertain about their first baby's ability to go off to sleep without their intervention.

In sum, if parents feel strongly that they wish to avoid night-waking beyond the first three months, it will be helpful for them over the initial weeks and months to observe their baby's manner of settling to sleep. The ease or difficulty that babies experience in making this transition varies enormously, and the particular strategies that are helpful to the baby are similarly varied. By matching the settling strategy to the baby's individual tendency to find particular kinds of stimulation either soothing or unsettling, the baby can be helped to develop her ability to fall asleep more easily and to resume sleep by herself in the night.

CHAPTER FIVE

DEVELOPING A SENSE OF SECURITY

DEVELOPING A SENSE OF SECURITY

The foundations for later security are laid in everyday, early experiences

Babies come to the world with a general readiness to engage socially with those around them, and they learn quickly about the personal characteristics of the members of their family. As the weeks and months go by, and the baby has repeated experiences of being cared for in particular ways, distinctive patterns of relating develop between the baby and the individuals who care for her.

These developing attachments involve strong emotions to do with dependency and security. A different pattern of attachment may develop between the baby and her mother, from that between the baby and her father or another adult who has been closely involved in her care. When that care is given through the early months in a consistent and reliable way that is sensitive to the baby's developing needs, the baby is likely to develop a sense of security in the relationship. So, in an unfamiliar environment she will feel safe in that person's presence and, if distressed, she will be able to be comforted by them. There is no intrinsic reason why the baby's attachment to her father, or other carer, should not be as secure as that to her mother; the nature of the attachment will depend on the quality of the interactions that take place with the baby.

As time goes on, the child who has benefited from security in her relationships with those who have cared for her is likely to develop a sense of self-confidence and assurance, so that she will have better resources to cope with difficulties. The signs of secure attachment become increasingly clear after about six to nine months, when, for example, the baby may become upset if the parent or other attachment figure leaves the room, but then greets them and settles easily on their return. But the foundations of these patterns of attachment are already being laid in the early months in the course of daily, repeated acts of care.

CHAPTER SIX

SUPPORTING PARENTS

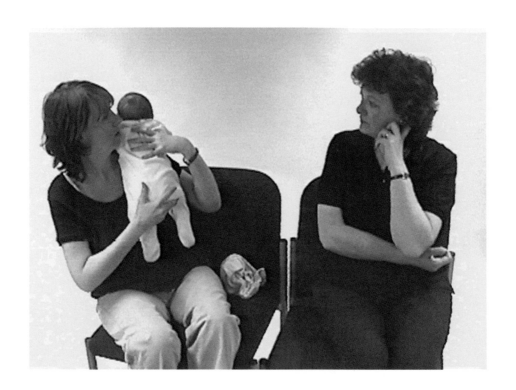

SUPPORTING PARENTS
Those caring for babies need care themselves

THE ROLE OF THE HEALTH VISITOR

Although Colette enjoys caring for her baby immensely, it can still be helpful to have the support of someone who can take the time to listen to the details of her experience with her daughter, Emily, and who can help to make sense of her baby's needs. Ideally, Health Visitors, like Liz, can fulfil this role; many have received additional training in counselling skills, in addition to their nursing and health visiting qualifications, and they provide a universal service to families with children under the age of five.

EMOTIONAL WELL-BEING

For the majority of families, caring for their young baby is a very positive experience. However, it is also an extremely demanding business, especially when the baby is one who cries a great deal, or who persistently wakes the parents at night. Studies in the UK and the US show that some 10-15% of mothers suffer from a period of depression in the weeks and months following childbirth. Women are at increased risk of postnatal depression if they have been prone to depression in the past, but a range of other factors are also important. Of central relevance are the degree of support the mother receives from her partner, and whether she has other people she can confide in and rely upon to give her help, her own mother's support being particularly important. The family's housing conditions, as well as the general suitability of the neighbourhood for child care, have also been found to relate to postnatal depression. Finally, the pressure to resume paid employment in the early postnatal months, whether out of financial necessity, or else to safeguard a valued career, also places a considerable burden on women at a time when they are particularly vulnerable. Fathers, too, can find the demands of having a new baby difficult. In fact, studies of the partners of women who are depressed have found that they are at increased risk of depression themselves. In sum, in order to be able to enjoy the demands of caring for a young baby, parents themselves need to be in a situation in which they are well cared for and feel secure.

THE ROLE OF HEALTH PROFESSIONALS

Although women have several contacts with health care professionals in the time around childbirth, many women's depression is not identified. Indeed, the mother herself may not realise that she is depressed. This may be particularly so for first-time mothers, who may not realise, for example, that the excessive fatigue or tearfulness they are feeling as part of their depression is not a normal part of the experience of early motherhood. They may, therefore, feel reluctant to bring these symptoms to the attention of their Health Visitor or GP. Unfortunately, it also has to be said that parents report that health care professionals are not always as supportive as they might be, even when a mother does bring her problems to their attention. This is particularly regrettable when one considers that there is good evidence that the majority of women who are postnatally depressed make a rapid recovery if they receive support from specially trained health care workers such as Health Visitors. New Government initiatives in the UK to support parents should bring about improvements in the care given by health professionals, and certainly, parents who feel they are not coping and who feel they may be depressed should feel that it is absolutely legitimate to ask for, and expect to receive, their help.

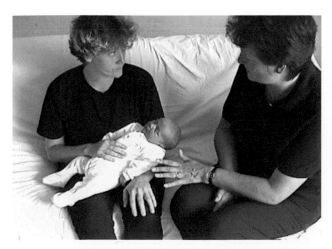

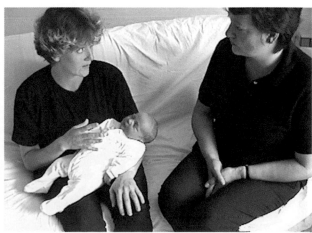

CHAPTER SEVEN

LIFESTYLES AND CHOICES

LIFESTYLE AND CHOICES
Matching the needs of babies, parents and society

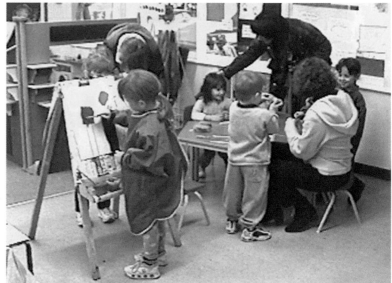

COMBINING EMPLOYMENT AND CARE FOR THE BABY

The situations facing parents when their children are born vary enormously, and people organise their lives around their children in many different ways. Decisions about particular arrangements for the care of the baby are influenced by a range of factors. The most obvious are financial, including salary, benefit and taxation provisions, as well as the timing and scale of statutory leave allowances and job protection. In recent years there has been a dramatic shift in the structure of the UK work force, with women (including those with young children) making up an increasing proportion of the labour market. Indeed, in some localities women may have more opportunities for work than men, although much of this may be part-time. Apart from such obvious economic influences on decisions about having children and the organisation of child care, there are also marked variations in personal preferences and beliefs regarding the balance of child care and paid work, and about the division of responsibilities between parents.

Across Europe, there is no one dominant pattern of preferred arrangement for balancing the care of children and paid work. Financial considerations aside, some parents feel strongly that they want to spend time at home with their children, and are committed to parenthood as their primary role. Others are just as strongly committed to their work and, while they want to have children and do their best by them, they feel that it is better to do this by focussing primarily (in terms of time) on their career. Others will want to give both work and the care of their children significant time and energy, the balance often shifting with the age of their children, with more time being spent at home early on.

Some European countries, particularly in Scandinavia, have parental leave provision, employment laws, and benefit and taxation policies that are highly supportive of parents who wish to stay at home for up to three years after the birth of their child. The position in the UK is changing, but at the time of writing, the comparable provisions appear to assume that mothers will return to work quickly (fathers' time at home is even more limited). This may be why British mothers have particularly fast rates of return to employment in the nine months following childbirth.

EFFECTS ON PARENTS AND BABIES OF EARLY RETURN TO EMPLOYMENT

Research findings have shown that, from the perspective of mothers, the emotional toll of returning to work full-time within the first four months after childbirth, and having the baby looked after by someone other than the father, is substantial. This holds true even when this is the parents' preferred child care arrangement, and when parental income is taken into account. Similarly, parents who feel there is no choice but for the father to spend long hours caring for the baby in the first few months, often already having done a day's work, so that the mother is released to take up employment, can experience considerable strain.

With regard to the impact of parental employment on early relationships between parents and their babies, there is evidence to suggest that a rapid return to work can pose difficulties. This is particularly likely in the case of babies who are sensitive, for whom the changes in routine and the additional adjustments required with different caretaking regimes, may be stressful. In addition, if an early return to work and prolonged use of non-parental care occurs in the context of other stresses (for example, financial problems), it can be more difficult for parents to engage responsively with their baby, possibly because they are not so familiar with her particular communication cues.

For those parents whose baby is cared for by other people, the quality of that care is important. Stable arrangements, with high ratios of caregivers to children, good morale and continuity of caregivers, are key elements that are likely to promote greater sensitivity to the child's needs.

Such standards are particularly important to child welfare and development in circumstances where parents, for whatever reason, are unable to provide good quality care themselves. These conditions may, however, demand a greater level of financial investment than parents alone are able to afford, and there is an important role for Governments to provide financial support for good quality care.

POLICY IMPLICATIONS

In terms of future policy, the needs of children are likely to be best met where there is scope for a variety of solutions that can meet the range of parental preferences about how family life and work are combined. Forcing parents into situations that are in fundamental conflict with their deeply held beliefs and personal values, whether that be to force them back to work shortly after childbirth, or to deny them access to valued careers if they take a substantial amount of time to care for their baby, is clearly not consistent with parental well-being. However, it is not just in the interests of parents that they should be well supported when they have a young baby. It is, of course, in the baby's best interests that her parents are not preoccupied by other worries, or are feeling exhausted and under stress; in these circumstances it can be hard to respond to the baby's communication and needs in a consistent and sensitive fashion. Policies to support parents in caring for their baby in the way they want are important, therefore, not least because they will be of long-term benefit to the baby herself.

The black and white book seen on pages 124–125, and the mobile used in *The Social Baby* can be purchased as a pack of four books and self-assembly mobile from all good bookshops.

Alternatively, purchases can be made online at our secure website www.cpshopping.co.uk, along with other books from The Children's Project. More information about The Children's Project is available at www.childrensproject.co.uk.